THE FIVE
GREAT RULES
OF SELLING

THE FIVE
GREAT RULES
OF SELLING

by

Percy H. Whiting

Managing Director
Dale Carnegie & Company

FIRST EDITION
Fourth Impression

New York : London

McGRAW-HILL BOOK COMPANY, INC.

1947

THE FIVE GREAT RULES OF SELLING

To
GENE

How This Book Came to Be Written

In the spring of 1939, Dale Carnegie decided to offer a course in selling, to supplement his course in effective speaking. He turned over to me the job of selecting a suitable textbook—a book that dug right into the basic fundamentals of selling.

I read most of the books offered by American publishers but found little that told a salesman not only what to do but *how to do it.*

So I wrote the book myself.

This is it!

PERCY H. WHITING

NEW YORK, N. Y.
August, 1947.

Why an Introduction?

The man who graduates today and stops learning tomorrow is uneducated the day after.

—Newton D. Baker.

If a book helps you, it introduces itself; if it doesn't, an introduction by G. B. Shaw wouldn't save it.

The purpose of this book is to help salesmen to sell. It is a "how to do" book. Many books in selling contain long lists of the qualities a salesman needs in order to be successful. "Be enthusiastic," they tell you. "Be brave."

But they don't tell you *how!*

This book gives only a brief list of needed qualities—but it tells you *how* to develop them.

It gives you only a few principles to apply to your selling activities—but it tells you *how* to apply them.

That's all of the introduction.

Contents

CHAPTER ONE

Most of This Chapter Is Omitted!

Salesmanship—That which makes you buy something you don't need when you ain't got the money to pay for it.

—WILL ROGERS.

Most books on salesmanship start off by defining the word "selling."

This book omits it.

Let's omit also a discussion of the economic importance of selling to the world of business and industry.

Let's not waste much time on the idea that the world never has had too many salesmen—and never will have.

If you can sell successfully you will not be out of a job for any long period. The harder times get, the more need there is for salesmen who can sell. I have heard of a dead organization that had enough salesmen but never of a live organization that had enough *good* salesmen.

How can you become a "good salesman"? Read on!

Selling Maxims *

If it is easy for you to sell, probably you will never become a great salesman.

* Many of the selling maxims in this book are not original. Credit is not given to the authors because they are unknown to me.

1

Learn from the school of experience if you must, but don't expect any recesses.

It's no disgrace to say, "I don't know," once or even twice. No alert salesman ever says it three times.

Be willing—eager—to learn. Bovee says: "He who is contented with what he has done will never be famous for what he will do. He has lain down to die and the grass is already growing over him."

CHAPTER TWO

The "How" of Selling

*The difference between the two groups [of insurance salesmen]—
the upper 25 per cent who do about 75 per cent of the business and
the lowest 25 per cent who just struggle along—is primarily a difference in the skill with which they do the job. The upper group is
distinguished by the pleasing way they tell the story to the public.*
—HOLGAR JOHNSON of the National Association of Underwriters.

In 1918, I was advertising manager of Central Maine Power
Company of Augusta. The company was trying to sell its
preferred stock in order to finance the building of a power
plant that was needed for war work. Its security-sales force
consisted of four demoted vacuum-cleaner salesmen and another man who wasn't any good either.

Sales were slow. One day the treasurer, Walter S. Wyman,
called me in and asked me to run some advertisements to
increase stock sales.

Nothing happened.

Sales didn't get any worse. That is one good feature of
sales—they can't go below zero. They can surely stay right
there a long time, though.

So Mr. Wyman suggested that I go down to Bath, where
the salesmen were working, and see if a pep talk would do
them any good.

I called a meeting of our entire sales force—all five of

them—and gave them what I supposed was an excellent pep talk. I told them how good my advertising was and how much stock they would sell if they would get behind it—but not too far behind!

When I had finished talking, a tall, gangling Yankee named Clarke got up and said, "Percy, if your advertising is so good that it practically sells the stock, why don't you go out and accept a few orders!"

Well, there I was in the selling business! Though I had never sold anything before in my life and had never so much as seen a stock certificate, in the ensuing two weeks I sold more stock than all the other members of the sales force put together. Yes, I sold seven shares—they didn't sell a share.

I was then the sixth worst salesman in the United States.

At the end of two weeks, Mr. Wyman came to me and said, "Percy, it is perfectly obvious to us all that you will never by any chance be a salesman, so we are going to make you sales manager."

Well, there I was with a lot of responsibility and no experience or knowledge or skill. So I bought every book on selling I could find.

The secretary of the Library of Congress wrote me in March, 1941, that the Library owned slightly over 1,000 books and booklets on selling. I do not claim to have read them all, but I do believe that in those years when I was a sales manager I read all the important books on selling that were published, and I know that I read regularly all the important sales and advertising magazines.

In that period I supervised the training of 72,000 men and women to sell. As I learned a new idea from a book or a salesman or through my own work in the field, I got my salesmen to try it out. I was thus able to give the idea a large-scale test and to find out quickly whether or not it worked.

As a result of this study, testing, and experience, I have arrived at these conclusions:

1. Just five rules of selling are vital. Not even a score are important and not over a scant hundred are even worth recording.

2. Nothing new has been discovered about selling in the last hundred years.

3. What salesmen need is not a lot of rules or a dose of fine-spun psychology, but to learn a few basic principles of selling and to be drilled in these principles until they habitually apply them to their selling problems.

You Get a Few Well-tested Rules

I shall give you only a few rules. They are the rules that through a fifth of a century have worked for me and for 72,000 people whose sales training I supervised. I do not deny that in that time I tried a vast number of ideas that did not work. They failed and were thrown overboard. Thus the readers of this book can profit by the mistakes of others— and at their expense.

Are these rules new?

No! The youngest of them is probably a thousand years old.

Salesmen don't need new rules. They need to learn the old ones—and to apply them.

"If I follow these rules, can I sell successfully?" you ask.

The answer is, "Not necessarily." If you follow the rules

you will be a *better* salesman, but you may not be good enough to make a living at selling.

My old friend T. E. Falvey used to phrase it this way: "Everybody in the world is either a salesman or a book-keeper." What he meant by that was that some people are congenitally unfitted to be successful salesmen.

I subscribe to the belief that there is such a thing as a natural-born salesman. When I was in charge of a large security organization we had a salesman in Ohio who was always near the top in production, yet he boasted that he didn't know one rule of selling. Just for curiosity, I sent a man out to make some calls with him. I found, as I had expected, that he was observing most of the important rules—but that he was doing so because he was born with a knack of selling.

The important men in almost any sales organization are not the "naturals" but the men who are fair salesmen now and can be improved. If these men will learn a few simple rules and then consciously apply them until they learn to apply them automatically, they will increase their sales volume astonishingly.

No Man Is a Failure Unless He Uses These Rules—and Still Can't Sell

Many men who are struggling along today with low morale and no enthusiasm can be transformed, by the application of these rules, into successful salesmen.

Take the case of John L. Batdorff, a real estate salesman of Cleveland. He took the Dale Carnegie Institute public speaking course. The first week he took the course he tried some of the rules he had learned from reading "How to Win

Friends and Influence People." In that week he sold three pieces of residence property—the most he had ever sold in one week in his eighteen years of selling. In the first month after he started the course he earned more commissions than in all twelve months of the previous year.

Let no man decide he is not a born salesman until he has tried these rules in his day-to-day work. They have pulled literally tens of thousands of men out of the mire of failure and have magically transformed them into successful salesmen.

Experience with 72,000 people has proved to me that any salesman, good or bad, who learns these rules and applies them will increase his sales volume. This is just as true of you as it is of all the others. It worked for them, it will work for you.

Selling Maxims

A lot of salesmen say, "Yes, I always knew that," and hence never learn anything.

Three dangerous "dones": It's never been done, It can't be done, and It's been overdone.

Your knowledge can't go much beyond your experience—so try everything.

"What you do when you don't have to determines what you will be when you can't help it."

The "naturals" were not taught, they were just born. The rest of us have to be both born and taught.

"The recipe for perpetual ignorance is to be satisfied with your opinions and content with your knowledge."—ELBERT HUBBARD.

Are you a better salesman today than you were yesterday? If not, you will be a still worse one tomorrow.

To paraphrase Elbert Hubbard: "Selling is not a *thing*, it is a way."

CHAPTER THREE

Making Habit Your Slave

Men acquire a particular quality by constantly acting in a particular way.

—ARISTOTLE.

The night before this chapter was written, I was teaching the last session of a fourteen-session Carnegie selling course. As the session opened, I asked the class to give me the rule for arousing interest. They had had one entire session of drill on this rule. Yet not one man out of twenty-five could give it. Only two out of the twenty-five could even approximate it.

One student spoke up and said: "We can't give the rule, but we use it." I did not believe him then and I don't believe him now.

Not one of those twenty-five men could use the rule for arousing interest—because not one of them knew it.

How can you avoid making that mistake? How can you make the selling rules in this book a part of your selling equipment? By the same technique you used in learning, for example, to shift gears. Here are the steps you used in learning to shift:

1. Somebody told you how.
2. You memorized the rule.
3. You consciously put the rule in practice. You told yourself: "Clutch out—step on that pedal. Then shove this lever

9

forward and to the right. Then let the clutch back in by taking my foot off that pedal. And remember to take it off slowly or it will grab."

4. You kept on doing it consciously until all at once, and to your surprise, your subconscious mind came to your rescue. You have shifted gears automatically from that day to this.

You learn to apply the rules of selling in just this way: (*a*) You memorize the rule. (*b*) You drill yourself on it until you do it automatically.

You cannot easily learn to use rules in any other way.

Teach yourself these rules, one at a time, by drill. Merely to *read* a book on selling is a waste of time. Why know the rules for arousing interest—or developing desire—unless you use them!

Make up your mind to this—and I repeat—you cannot easily and certainly learn how to use rules or a formula except by *drill*.

How You Learn to Use These Rules

How do you go about making the rules in this book part of your selling equipment?

You take the same steps that you did when you learned to shift gears, as follows:

1. Work on one rule at a time.
2. Memorize it.
3. Then consciously put the rule in practice.
4. Keep on doing it until it becomes second nature—until you do it automatically.
5. Then move on to the next one.

To try this, take a minor rule of answering objections:

"Start your answer by agreeing with your prospect about something." How do you make it part of your selling technique?

(*a*) You memorize it.

(*b*) You consciously put it in practice. For example, your prospect raises an objection. You say to yourself: "All right, the rule I am working on today is to start off answering each objection by agreeing with the prospect about something. So I'll say, 'I'm glad you brought up that point, Mr. Blank. I know just how you feel.' "

(*c*) You keep on using that technique until you do it automatically—without thinking.

Then you go on to the next rule.

Put Away Your Shotgun—Use a Rifle

Let me emphasize this rule: Work on only one rule at a time. Don't try to learn and put into use several rules at one time. Use a rifle—not a shotgun.

For example, I heard a student in a public-speaking class say this: "I read 'How to Win Friends and Influence People' in one night before I went to sleep. I resolved to lead a better life. When I woke up the next morning, I knew I meant to do something that day—but I had forgotten what. A week later, I reread the book. Then I tried a new plan. I took just one rule —and I took pains to remind myself continually that I was working on that rule. I started off with 'Don't criticize.' I worked one solid month on that rule, until it became a part of me not to criticize. Does that seem a long time? Well, remember, I had been criticizing for fifty years—so thirty days to learn how not to criticize was relatively quick work."

Take the rule for getting attention. Learn it, use it consciously day after day for a week at least. By that time it ought to be as natural as walking or eating. Then try the rule for arousing interest—and so on through the book.

The other day I read a book entitled "How to Remember." I told myself, "I'll read it all through first. Then I'll come back and try some of the rules." But alas, I forgot to go back —and I forgot where I put the book.

Don't be as stupid as I am. Don't wait to read the whole book before you start your course in self-improvement. Keep on reading the book but grab Rule 1 and start work on it tomorrow. Work on it a week at least. Then take Rule 2.

This is the best, easiest, and quickest way. Why use any other!

Maxims

"Any man may make a mistake; none but a fool will persist in it."—MARCUS CATO.

"Cultivate only the habits that you are willing should master you."—ELBERT HUBBARD.

"Practice is everything."—PERIANDER.

"Knowledge is a treasure, but practice is the key to it."— THOMAS FULLER.

CHAPTER FOUR

The Five Steps
of the Selling Process

He who is unready today will be more so tomorrow.
—OVID.

We shall use in this book the old, conventional steps of the selling process:

1. Gain your prospect's attention.
2. Arouse the interest of your prospect.
3. Convince your prospect that it is an intelligent move to buy your goods or service.
4. Arouse your prospect's desire to buy.
5. Close the sale successfully.

Or, to put it briefly: (1) Attention. (2) Interest. (3) Conviction. (4) Desire. (5) Close.

Unless you get your prospect's attention, why make your sales talk? You want him to keep on attending, so you get his interest.

Next you must convince him that it will be a wise move for him to buy—an intelligent thing to do.

He may be interested in your product, may be convinced that it is a good article, and still not do a thing about it. (You are interested, for example, in the Grand Canyon. You are convinced that no better canyon exists—but still you don't want it.) Therefore, after you have interested your prospect

13

and convinced him, you must make him *want* to own it before you can make the sale. That is, you must arouse desire.

Even if he is convinced that your product is as good as you claim, even if he wants it, he may not sign the order blank. So the next step is to close.

You may not always take your sales steps in the order given above. Also, you may often be able to skip some of the steps. For example, the prospect may be familiar with your product, may feel that it is the best on the market. In this case you may skip the conviction step. Once in a great while a prospect may, before you talk to him, have taken all the steps except closing, perhaps as a result of reading advertisements. This happens with considerable regularity in the automobile business, where, it is estimated, 65 per cent of all cars are not *sold*, but *bought*.

However, in learning to sell—or to sell more—we shall assume that a sale goes through the five steps—attention, interest, conviction, desire, close. If you cannot say this formula forward and backward, you should learn to do so right now. You will want to use it the rest of your life.

The five great rules of selling are the rules for carrying your prospect through these five steps of the sale.

Maxims

"He that will not be counselled cannot be helped."— THOMAS FULLER.

If you are satisfied to be "just a fair salesman," you'll never be even "just a fair salesman."

To paraphrase Sir James Barrie: "Selling is not really work, unless you would rather be doing something else."

Why look around for new selling methods until you have tried the old?

All of us think we could make a success of selling, if we only had time!

Do you find selling dull? Then try to find a better way to sell.

If your salesmanship is good, your sales will look after themselves.

"Make every sales talk as if it were your last," as Marcus Aurelius would say today.

CHAPTER FIVE

How to Gain Favorable Attention

Every living creature loves itself.
—CICERO.

Great Rule 1: *Get your prospect's attention by talking to him briefly about something in which he is interested.*

I should blush to call a rule so idiotically simple and obvious as this a "great rule"—if I had not, in my life, heard many thousands of sales talks that violated it. They were not all in the class of these two classics: "You don't want any today, do you?" and "Nice weather we're having"; but most of them were weak on attention-getting power. They were either remarks that interested the salesmen rather than the prospects—or remarks that did not interest anybody.

Before you approach your prospect, ask yourself, "In what feature of my product or service will he be interested?"

Of one thing you are sure: he is interested in himself. So some form of sincere compliment is the safest and best general-purpose, heavy-duty attention getter. For instance: "Congratulations on winning that golf tournament, Mr. Blank," or "That's a wonderful desk you have, Mr. Blank," or "I expected to find a much older man, Mr. Jones" (sure-fire if the man is past fifty—and the remark is sincere). Remember, mothers are always proud of their children; doctors and dentists of their office equipment; businessmen of their offices;

16

neat men of neat desks; disorderly men of disorderly desks; purchasing agents of their efficient buying; old men of their youth; and young men of their age.

An Honest and Sincere Compliment—and It Worked!

One day I was calling on an important official of an A. T. and T. subsidiary in upstate New York. When I reached this man's desk I said, "On my way up to see you, Mr. Blank, I had to ask the way of five of your employees— and every one of them gave me a big smile."

He responded with the biggest smile in the lot and replied, "If you knew how long and hard I have worked to get our employees to greet people with a smile, you would know how I appreciate that compliment"—and I was off to a good start.

Keep your eyes open when you go into a man's office or store in an effort to discover something you can honestly compliment. Especially watch for something new and different. A man's million-dollar store may be old stuff to him, while a new back door may occupy, at the moment, a place of great importance in his mind.

If you can make your attention getter something that leads naturally into your sales talk, so much the better.

Other Ways of Getting Attention

The sincere compliment is a good attention getter for any salesman to use any time; but it is by no means the only crasher available.

For convenience, I am dividing attention getters into those useful to specialty salesmen and those applicable to jobbers' salesmen. Many of them can be used to advantage by retail salesmen.

Openers for Specialty Salesmen

Don't get into the rut of using just one kind of opener—not, at least, until you have tried them all and learned which is the most effective. Here are some suggestions for the salesman who is selling a specialty:

1. The Question Opener. This is one of the easiest and most effective of openers. If your prospect answers the question he must pay attention.

For example, a laundry company equipped its route men with big badges on which appeared the question: "Can you drink it?" It got attention by arousing curiosity.

Insurance men use a table that shows the "money value" of a man and get attention for it by asking, "Do you know that insurance companies limit the amount of insurance they will let you buy?"

2. The Startling Statement or "Explosion" Type of Opener. A punch line can be an effective crasher. So can a startling statement, if it really is startling and if it is unknown to your prospect and if it is directly applicable to what you are selling.

An insurance salesman opened his talk by pulling a pencil from his pocket, breaking it in half, throwing the pieces on the floor, and saying, "You can't do it with a lead pencil. Figuring won't support your wife—not if you die without insurance."

A Scott paper-towel salesman used this startling statement: "I never saw a paper towel worth a hoot!" Then he explained the difference between Scott towels and ordinary paper towels.

HOW TO GAIN FAVORABLE ATTENTION   19

3. The Interest Getter, or "Why Bring This Up," Opener.
When you use this opener you bring part of your interest step
into the opening of your sales talk. That is, you immediately
tell your prospect why your goods or service will benefit him.

Example: "These vending machines will increase your sale of
. . . and hence your profits."

4. The Illustration, or "For Instance," Opener. If you have
a really striking example that you would normally use somewhere in the body of your sales talk, pull it out of its normal
position and start with it. In other words, start by telling
a story—one of the natural and unfailing methods of getting
attention.

Example: John Smith, 234 Smith Street, Smithville, Missouri, kept
a record for one month on the time his secretary wasted waiting for
dictation while he was answering the telephone. It averaged one hour
and twenty-three minutes a day. It cost him $340 a year.

5. The Mysterious, or "Believe It or Not," Opener. In this
case you arouse your prospect's curiosity by your opening
remarks, and keep it aroused at least through the beginning
of your talk. This is one of the most effective possible attention getters. If the prospect says to himself, "I wonder what
this salesman is driving at?" you surely have his attention.

Some years ago a man hired the opera house in a small Pennsylvania town for one night, but engaged no ushers or other staff. About
a month before the date for which he had rented the hall, he put a
large sign on the most prominent billboard in town, stating in huge
letters: "He Is Coming!"
A week before the fateful night, this was replaced by: "He Will
Be at the Opera House on October 31!" The day before the event
there was the simple legend: "He Is Here!" The following morning,
"He Will Be at the Opera House Tonight at 8:30!"

That night the man himself sat in the box office and sold tickets at $1 a head to a capacity audience. When the lights went up inside, however, all the crowd could see was a huge sign reading: "He Is Gone!"

—WALTER WINCHELL quoting S. J. KAUFMAN.

Such a technique arouses curiosity, but it would hardly be effective in a sales talk! Suppose, however, you called on a sales manager and fired these questions at him.

"Did you ever happen to listen to one of your salesmen making a sales talk—when he didn't know you were listening? Was he saying what you wanted him to say—the way you wanted him to say it? For your advertising you list eleven sales points for your product—do you know how many of them the salesmen are using in their sales talks? Do you realize you can spend a million dollars for modern sales training and still not get your salesmen to say what you want them to say?"

At this point you might not have your prospect thrilled, but you would certainly have him wondering what you were talking about and why—and you are better off than if he were not even wondering.

This "believe it or not" opener calls for ingenuity but it can be extremely effective. A variety of this opener is the curiosity arouser.

Here is an example: Charles Moore, an insurance salesman in Memphis, has nothing on his card except his name and the letters "C.L.U." Mr. Moore says that nine out of ten of his prospects ask him what the meaning of C.L.U. is. He then explains to them that it is a degree, Chartered Life Underwriter, given by the American College of Life Underwriters, which is subsidized by the major life insurance companies. He adds that there are only five life insurance salesmen in Memphis who are qualified to hold this degree. Thus the prospect has actually asked Charles to tell him just how good he is and has launched him in his sales talk!

Another example: A catsup salesman walks into a store and asks for "a bottle of your best catsup." He opens it, whips out a spoon, and asks the grocer to taste it. Next he brings a bottle of his own catsup out of his pocket and asks the grocer to try that.

Quite obviously, he has the prospect's attention by this performance.

From *The Postage Stamp* magazine comes this example of getting attention by arousing curiosity:

Tom Lowry, before his death some years ago, was known beyond the limits of his home city, Milwaukee, as a utility tycoon—and as a man in whom the gambling urge was well developed.

He was also known to insurance agents as the man who couldn't be sold.

Then an up-and-coming young agent decided he was going to sell Tom Lowry. He learned, of course, that Lowry was the sort of man who would bet on the way a hop-toad would hop. The solicitor strode into the great man's outer office and said he wanted to see Mr. Lowry about a bet. He was immediately admitted.

"Mr. Lowry, I'll bet you $100,000 to $1,800 that you'll not die within the next year."

Insurance hadn't been presented to Tom Lowry like that before. He took the bet.

6. The Famous-man, or Big-name, Opener. If you say, "John Smith thinks our machine is the best in the world," it is not a striking utterance; but if you can say, "Henry Ford told one of our salesmen that . . .," you get attention by the use of a big name.

7. The Screw-driver Opener. If you sell something that may need servicing, an effective opener is to start in by looking over your prospect's equipment—and making any needed adjustment or screw-driver repairs. From *The Howe Salesmen* come these suggestions: "Carry a screw driver with you. And a can of metal polish. And a piece of polishing cloth. Approach the prospect with a suggestion that you'd like to look over his scales and see if they are working all right. . . . Use the metal polish and polishing cloth on the scale beam. Adjust the balance ball, if it needs it. . . . Twirl the wheel of a truck. If it runs sluggishly, ask for an oilcan and drop some oil on the axle."

By the time you have done a few acts of service, you have attention—and perhaps a number of facts that will help you later in your sales talk.

8. The Exhibit, or "Here We Have," Attention Getter. If your product is one that provides you with a good exhibit of some kind, be sure to use it. A salesman talking to a group of people one night opened with the statement, "This little gadget may revolutionize the world." He then exhibited an electric eye, which at that time was quite new. You may well believe that he had the attention of everyone present.

We used to supply our preferred-stock salesmen, when I was directing the sales for a small power company, with short pieces of high-tension copper wire. The salesman would place a piece in the hands of a prospect and ask him if he realized what a miracle it was that all the power furnished to his city was brought there along strands of wire just like that. Later, when the company switched to aluminum wire, then quite new in that section, we supplied pieces of aluminum wire to salesmen and told them to hand it to their prospects and ask them if they knew what it was. In the second case, we not only used an exhibit but also took advantage of one of the great attention arousers, curiosity.

Insurance salesmen frequently supply themselves with clippings about deaths or accidents, which they place before the prospect—another form of "exhibit."

Norvall Hawkins recommends that attention be secured by "making direct sense appeals in an unusual manner."

The salesmen who used the copper or aluminum wire appealed to the senses of sight and touch. The man who peddles little head-shaking, tail-wagging Scotties on the street appeals to your hearing by whistling, barking, or making some other noise to attract your attention. Demonstrators in drugstores offer perfume to you to smell.

One life insurance salesman introduces himself by saying, "Mr. Blank, I sell money for future delivery—here is my business card," and hands the prospect a crisp dollar bill.

Attention Getters That Jobbers' Salesmen Can Use

"So you're here again" is the best greeting that a lot of jobbers' salesmen deserve from customers.

Don't be satisfied with that sort of greeting. How avoid it? By being interesting or helpful—and by wasting no time in getting to the point.

1. The News Item, or "It Just Happened," Attention Getter. Become a traveling newsgathering bureau. Read trade papers and magazines, read papers from other cities, and get news items out of them. Remember the news that dealers give you.

A grand opening phrase is, "I just heard that. . . ."

If it's news, it's interesting.

Example: When I was doing some work for a chain-store group, a man came in one day and said, "The Colorado Supreme Court has just rendered a verdict that lumps voluntary chains with regular chains and makes them both liable for chain-store taxes." Because this was exciting news to me that day, the salesman had my full and interested attention.

(Warning: Be careful about passing around news about competitors to competitors. Don't tell secrets or violate confidences.)

2. Helpful Suggestions. Of course the salesman who brings suggestions that increase sales for the dealer is more than welcome. And of course the man with helpful suggestions gets immediate interest. So your job is to get yourself in a position where you can give suggestions. They will probably fall in one of these classifications:

(*a*) *Advertising Ideas.* If you start talking to a dealer of poultry supplies with these words, you are likely to get attention: "John Smith, up in Smithville, wrote this advertisement himself and ran it in the local paper at a cost of $25. It brought him seventeen incubator sales. I have some extra copies if you'd like one."

If you are a jobber's salesman, your company probably supplies you with plenty of advertising copy. One of your jobs is to find out how a given piece of copy has worked for one merchant, so you can tell another.

To say to a merchant, "My company thinks this is a good advertisement," is not impressive. If you say, "John Smith ran this advertisement at a cost of $25 and made sales of $450," you have real attention.

Try to be a helpful adviser to your customers. Try to find which advertisements really pull and pay. Then tell your customers about them.

(*b*) *Selling Ideas.* If you are a salesman, your company doubtless gives you selling ideas. You probably hear them

from customers. You can get them from books. But do you
make a practice of passing them along? You should.

What sort of ideas? Anything that helps the merchant to
sell your product—or any product except your competitors'.

Other Promotion Ideas

Dealers will welcome any man who can show them how
to make more money. If the company has produced a new
mailing piece or a selling idea, it is often wiser to let the
salesman, rather than the mailman, peddle it.

Ray Giles, in *Advertising and Selling*, made this practical
suggestion for the use of a ". . . well-filled loose-leaf binder,
copies of which are left with active accounts and the better
prospective customers. The pages inside contain digests of
good retail selling methods assembled from various sources:
business publications, field experience, and promising experiments suggested by the sales promotion department.

"The material is put in a loose-leaf binder to help build a
welcome for the salesman from call to call. First of all he
asks for the binder and inserts additional pages, explaining
briefly what they're about and why they should be studied.
Thus every sales interview becomes also a servicing operation."

CHAPTER SIX

Additional Rules for Gaining Attention

I to myself am dearer than a friend.
—SHAKESPEARE.

Rule 1: Carefully prepare your attention-getting remarks before you come face to face with your prospect.

Elmer Wheeler, in his book "Tested Sentences That Sell," says, "The first ten words are more important than your next ten thousand." An exaggeration, of course—but an effective one.

Rule 2: Never start with an apology. In fact the old rule: "Never apologize, never explain, never retract, get it done, and let 'em holler," is worth thinking about—even if you don't follow it unfailingly.

You are doing the prospect a favor when you give him the facts about your product. *Radio Jobbers News* quotes a successful radio-parts distributor as saying, "But for the persistence of salesmen, I might not today have many of my good selling lines. I learn many things from them. As I see it, they help me to keep my job."

Rule 3: Never ask for "a few minutes of your time." Sometimes, in dealing with a man who is very busy—or thinks he is—you can put your watch in front of you and say, "If I haven't interested you in five minutes, I'll leave." If you make that statement, stick to it.

Rule 4: Get your prospect saying Yes. This is not so important as some salesmen seem to think, yet it is good technique. It is usually quite as easy to get Yes answers as No answers. For example: "Is it all right if I hang my hat here?" "You have an amazing view out of this window, haven't you?" "You can be proud of having offices in a building like this, can't you?"

Rule 5: Don't, I implore you, *don't* use the "I just happened by" introduction. If you haven't a better reason than that for calling, don't call.

Rule 6: Make your attention getter brief. If you spin it out you may first get attention and next lose it. Often one sentence or one question is enough. Why? Because you can't hold attention long.

Hugo Münsterberg of Harvard used to illustrate the point that attention is hard to hold by telling of the alchemist who sold a recipe for turning eggs into gold. The buyer was to put the yolks of a dozen eggs into a pan and stir these yolks for a half hour without ever thinking of the word "hippopotamus." Thousands tried but none succeeded.

If people can't keep their attention on one thing for thirty minutes for a pan of gold, they aren't likely to succeed for the privilege of listening to your sales talk. So get attention quickly—and press on to the interest step of your talk.

He Never Got Down to His Sales Talk

F. W. Nichols, then vice-president and general manager of International Business Machines, tells this story:

A friend of mine was talking to a visitor in his office the other day when a salesman was announced. My friend said that, just as a demonstration, he would give the salesman five minutes of his time.

The visitor pushed back his chair and relaxed to watch the demonstration. The salesman was asked in.

As soon as he entered, the executive began talking about the general economic situation, golf, and other subjects. The salesman responded in a like vein. At the end of the fifth minute the executive said: "Well, nice of you to call on me. I enjoyed meeting you. Thank you very much." And so the salesman was shown out. He had not, despite the opportunity offered him, said a word as to why he had come.

How can you switch over a general conversation into the serious subject of selling your goods? Herbert N. Casson once answered this question thus: "Ask the buyer questions that relate to your goods. This keeps the buyer talking but it makes him talk on the right subject."

Rule 7: Never force your prospect to shake hands. If he seems to expect it, shake; if not, don't.

Rule 8: Try to sit or stand reasonably close to your prospect. On the other hand, don't get too close. Your breath may have some bearing on the distance you should sit from your prospect. If it is sweet, don't worry. If it is bad, don't sit too close. (Also, if it is bad, do something about it. Don't eat so much, don't eat so fast, chew more carefully, avoid onions and garlic—and, if that doesn't cure you, see a doctor.)

Rule 9: Don't loll in your chair. You should have a message of importance for your prospect and should act accordingly. Sit or stand straight.

Rule 10: In general, do not smoke while you are selling. There are exceptions, of course. But if in doubt, don't. Also, don't drink (if you must drink at all) until after your last sales call. Some hard drinkers and most teetotalers hate to talk to a man with a liquor breath.

Rule 11: Avoid talking to your prospect when others—especially uninterested people—are present. If you find a third person present, you can say to your prospect: "Pardon me, I did not know that you were engaged. When will you be able to see me?" This frequently causes the undesirable third person to withdraw—or gives you another date for the interview.

If you have to talk in the presence of a gallery, talk not to one person but to all of them.

Selling All Over the Lot

I recall that once I made a night call on a prospect who lived in the country a few miles north of Augusta, Maine. My prospect was the grandmother of a large family who lived in a big, sprawling farmhouse. I started talking to the grandmother. Soon the daughter and granddaughter came in and sat down in different parts of the big living room. They clearly expected to be included, so I raised my voice and talked to them too. Pretty soon grandfather and the hired man came in and sat down in the adjoining kitchen. They were entirely out of my sight, but after grandfather asked a question, I had to include them. Then, to make it perfect, a maiden aunt who had been napping in a bed room, which was off the opposite end of the living room, waked up and asked a question. So, for the remainder of the talk, I was addressing six people seated in three rooms—and half of them entirely out of my sight. I got the order but I almost wrecked my nervous system.

Rule 12: Smile. You *can* learn to do it naturally and effec-

tively. I nearly learned to do it myself—in seventeen years.
Most people accomplish it faster! You do it by "thinking a
smile." Before you go in to see your prospect say to yourself,
"I make my living by selling people. I like people—if I didn't
I wouldn't sell. I am going to like this man. It's a good world.
I have my health and a lot of other blessings. Surely I feel
like smiling."

Don't dismiss this as foolishness. It works.

A Smile Made Him a Champion Salesman

Does smiling pay salesmen? At a Dale Carnegie Institute
class session in Boston a girl told this story:

Several years ago a small boy walked into my office one day and
said dolefully, "Want to buy a *Saturday Evening Post?*" I said "No.
I'm busy." So he went out. On my way out to lunch I met the lad
at the elevator, and I asked him if he had sold any *Posts*. He said he
hadn't. So I said, "I'm no salesman but I'll give you one rule. When
you say 'Want to buy a *Post?*' you smile."

One week later this boy breezed into my office, gave me a big
smile and said, "Want to buy a *Post?*" Almost unconsciously I
reached for my purse and handed him a nickel.

Soon that boy led all *Post* boys in the Boston area. He was a
leader until he grew too big to peddle magazines. Many times he has
told me, "I owe it all to my smile."

On the other hand, don't be a perpetual smirker. After the smile
of courtesy, get down to business and look businesslike.

Rule 13: Don't start your sales talk as soon as you pop
your head in the door, as you walk to your prospect's desk,
or as you sit down. It makes your talk seem unimportant.
Your job is to make your sales talk seem *important*.

Avoid the Too Sensational Opener

Rule 14: Don't try to be too clever in your opening. A good friendly remark is safer than shooting off a skyrocket or standing on your head.

John Singer Sargent, the great portrait painter, used to have difficulty in getting and holding the attention of children whose portraits he was painting. So, he hit on the scheme of painting his own nose with red paint. This held the children spellbound. However, this plan is not recommended for salesmen.

I remember once a man came to my office at 72 Wall Street and opened his talk by asking, "What did your grandmothers die of?" I never did find out what he was selling—I just let him out.

Rule 15: Get the prospect's name right. You will get attention if you mispronounce it—but the wrong kind! Don't hesitate to ask your prospect how to spell his name—your interest in his name will please him. If it is an unusual name, comment on that.

The other day, I overheard a salesman compliment a man on his unusual name. The man swelled with pride. "I'm the only one in the Manhattan telephone book," he said.

How to Get Back to Your Prospect's Office

Rule 16: Use every reasonable effort to avoid making your talk on the doorstep, in the front of the store or office, or in a waiting room. Say to your prospect, "Do you mind if we step into your office?"—and start walking in that direction.

Another plan is to say, "Are you too busy now to go back into your office, Mr. Blank? If so, I'll be glad to come in later."

Then if the prospect still stands waiting for you to begin, say, "If you're too busy to have me go back with you now, I'll wait here, Mr. Blank."

A good many prospects will then invite you back to their desks, just to save their pride.

Often, however, one will say, "Go ahead—we can talk right here!"

If the prospect says, "I'll talk to you right here," you are justified in saying firmly, "Mr. Blank, I want only about three minutes of your time, but I want it back there at your desk, where we can talk without being disturbed. Will you give me that much?"

It is a pretty cranky man who can refuse under such circumstances.

Lastly, remember: grabbing attention is easy, holding it is difficult. Attention can be kept fixed only if it is kept moving.

Which brings us to the Second Great Rule of Selling—the rule for keeping attention fixed through converting it into interest.

CHAPTER SEVEN

How to Arouse a Prospect's Interest

Selling, to be a great art, must involve a genuine interest in the other person's needs. Otherwise it is only a subtle, civilized way of pointing a gun and forcing one into a temporary surrender.

—H. A. OVERSTREET.

Great Rule 2: *Arouse your prospect's interest by telling him what your goods or services will do to benefit or serve him.*

I was walking through a sporting-goods store when a clerk I know said, "Mr. Whiting, this is an odd-looking putter, isn't it?"

I glanced at it and said, "Yes, isn't it?" and passed on.

But suppose he had said, "Mr. Whiting, you know those long putts you are missing? Well, here's a putter that will sink them for you." I wouldn't have believed him, but I'd have stopped!

Why should your prospect listen to your sales talk?

If more salesmen would ask themselves this question and answer it, more sales would be made. Many salesmen seem to think that they have some God-given right to take the prospect's time. "But," protests the salesman, "why shouldn't I take his time? I'm here to do this man a service—to sell him something he really needs." True, I hope. But does the prospect know it? Does he know any reason why he should listen, why he should be interested?

In most cases, your prospect feels as Voltaire did about an unwelcome visitor, to whom he said, "Monsieur, I know absolutely nothing about any single question you are going to ask me."

Your prospect's natural and justifiable attitude is, "I don't want anything you are selling." He keeps feeling that way until you show him that what you are offering him will benefit or serve *him*.

In What Are Your Prospects Interested?

How can you know your prospect's interest?

In what one subject are we all interested? Ourselves. Hence, to interest anyone, talk to him about *himself*. Since you are there to make a sale, talk to the prospect about how your goods *will serve him*. To put it another way, talk about your goods in terms of your prospect's interests.

For example, if you are selling duplicating machines you might open your talk by saying, "I've come to sell you a duplicating machine"—but I hope you wouldn't! Suppose you say instead, "I believe I can show you how you can save over $500 a year on your form letters." In that case your prospect is likely to be interested.

This rule seems so obvious—so in accord with good psychology and good sense—that you may wonder why I stress it. If you have ever trained salesmen in thousand lots, as I have, you will realize that it is only by threats, rewards, drills, cajoling, and abuse that you can get one salesman out of a hundred to make it a regular practice to arouse interest before he begins to state the facts about his product.

This rule for arousing interest is as old as civilization— probably older.

One of the first men to use it in an advertisement was Benjamin Franklin. He tells about it in his autobiography, which is required reading for all ambitious salesmen. Back in April, 1755, Franklin was commissioned by General Braddock to secure for him 150 wagons with four horses to each wagon. These the general wanted for what proved to be his ill-fated expedition against Fort Duquesne.

Franklin went to Lancaster, and on Apr. 26, 1755, published an advertisement. The purpose of the advertisement was to get the farmers interested in supplying the wagons. What did it contain? One single paragraph about what Braddock wanted and six numbered paragraphs about what the farmers would get. In other words, good salesman that he was, Franklin told the farmers how they would benefit from the transaction.

Franklin comments on the "great and sudden effect it produced" and says further, "In three weeks the one hundred and fifty wagons, with two hundred and fifty-nine carrying horses, were on their march for the camp."

Suppose that instead of arousing the interest of the farmers in what they would get out of it, Franklin had told them what Braddock wanted—would he have secured equally good results? We don't have to guess. Braddock did try it in Maryland, on a "we want wagons or else" basis, just before he met Franklin. The net result, wrote Franklin, was ". . . twenty-five wagons and not all of those in serviceable condition."

It Takes Time to Prepare for Some Sales

The interest step in your sales talk may be as short as one sentence—or it may take a week or a year to prepare. If you are selling heavy machinery or complicated equipment you may have to spend weeks in a plant before you are ready to go beyond the interest step of your sales talk.

Sidney Carter in *Printers' Ink* gave this example of a man who spent weeks in his territory on the interest step before he really started selling.

A salesman selling oil and gas in a faraway state was a day behind his schedule the first week out. The second week he was two days behind. His sales manager wrote him and wired him urging him to get a move on. At the end of a month he was a week behind schedule. The sales manager sent him a hot wire which elicited this response: "Do you want me to sell your gasoline or burn it up? Letter follows." The letter explained that not one of the customers could recall the name of any of the company's previous representatives. The salesman added, "Give me time to get acquainted and build up something out here on a solid basis and I will sell gas." He is today the biggest producer for his company in the United States.

The editorial policy of *The Saturday Evening Post*, one of the great publishing successes of all the world for all time, is based on this belief: "The average American is interested in (*a*) his job, (*b*) his home [which presumably is meant to include his family], (*c*) his politics, (*d*) his recreation, (*e*) his health, (*f*) events of national interest."

The smart salesman may well be guided by this list. If you talk to your prospect about what service your goods will render him in connection with his job, his home, his recreation, or his health, you have talked to him about what is nearest his heart. *The Saturday Evening Post* used this list and grew rich. See if it will not make money for you.

Surely, then, the answer to your question, "How do I get the prospect interested in my goods?" can be easily answered: Tell your prospect how he will benefit from owning them. Remember, he wants to know not what your goods *are* but what they will *do* for *him*.

What If Your Product Has No Advantages?

"Yes," you say, "but every competitor can offer what I can—I sell just printing [or just sugar, or just pole-line hardware]. What can they do for my prospects that everybody else can't do, too?"

If, as can happen, your product has no real advantage over competing products, then your problem is one of human relations.

Generally, however, your product has advantages.

What are they? Your sales manager should be able to tell you. If not, dig them out before you make another call. Study your plant, study your product, study your service. Dig out the points in which your product excels. Find the ways in which *you* can render service to your customers.

Elbert Hubbard, back in the Roycrofters days, didn't sell "just printing." If he wrote the copy and the Roycrofters did the printing, the customers had something the like of which we had never seen before—or since.

Yes, But What about Purchasing Agents?

"That's all right," you say, "if you are selling direct to consumers. But I sell largely to purchasing agents. They don't benefit, no matter what they buy."

Many salesmen consider the purchasing agent as sort of a machine, into which are fed prices, specifications, terms, and the like, and out of which come decisions to buy from the salesman who offers the best combination of quality, price, service, and terms—usually with most of the emphasis on price.

That, of course, is not quite true. Actually, purchasing agents *are* human.

Take the hypothetical case of two salesmen of exactly equal ability who offer the same quality of goods at the same price and with the same service and terms—in competition with each other. Purchasing Agent A gives all his business to Salesman Y, while Purchasing Agent B gives it all to Salesman Z.

Why?

I don't know, but if I were Salesman Y or Salesman Z, I'd try hard to find out. Until you know the wants, lacks, needs, ambitions, and motives of purchasing agents, you cannot hope to tell them why they will benefit if they buy your line.

If you want to know how to sell to hard-to-sell purchasing agents, find out more about them. Then talk to them now and then about how they will benefit by buying from you. But remember, when price, terms, quality, and service are equal, the purchasing agent will usually buy from the salesman he likes to buy from. So part of your job is to improve your personality, so that you become the kind of salesman that purchasing agents like to deal with.

No Prospect Ever Wants to Buy Anything!

Beginners frequently feel that their prospects are sitting around, eager to buy and just waiting for the salesman to call. Then, when they find the prospect utterly uninterested, they become discouraged.

As a salesman gathers experience he changes his point of view. He knows that most prospects are utterly uninterested in what the salesman is selling—that they do not want to buy anything. The salesman then realizes that arousing interest by telling the prospect how the goods will serve him is a natural and necessary part of his sales talk.

Suppose an insurance salesman were to call on 1,000 people and ask each person, "Are you interested in buying some insurance?" Maybe one would say Yes, but surely 999 would say No. Until the insurance salesman has pointed out how insurance will benefit or serve the prospect, the prospect is not interested.

Therefore you don't sell insurance, you sell protection; you don't sell securities, you sell a means for retiring at sixty; you don't sell advertising space, you sell customers delivered at the store; you don't sell a rug, you sell a floor beautifully covered.

Leo McGivena wrote: "Last year over one million quarter-inch drills were sold—not because people wanted quarter-inch drills but because they wanted quarter-inch holes. When you buy an automobile you buy transportation. When you buy a mattress you are buying comfortable sleep. When you buy carbon paper you are buying copies."

"What will it do for me?" they ask. A story from *The Informant* illustrates this point.

A printing salesman, who called on a Swedish sawmill owner in Washington State, told the millman what wonderful printing his company did. Finally the shingle man said petulantly, "I don't want to buy printing—I like to sell shingle, you bet!"

"Why should anyone buy *your* shingles?" parried the salesman. The millman told him.

The salesman left but was back in two days with copy and layout for a $225 job. And the gentleman from Sweden bought it with these words, "Aye tank you smart fella—Aye gamble."

Sometimes you can interest your prospect not by telling him how your goods will benefit him—but how he can be benefited otherwise—by some selling idea that works, some display stunt, some advertisement, some scheme for better merchandising.

Lewis Greene Bissing was quoted in *American Business* as follows:

Most people think selling is so hard. . . . I claim it is easy when the salesman's goal is to do something for his customers. Not long ago a wholesaler asked us to call on a druggist with him.

I motioned to our factory man to do the talking when he met the druggist. First thing he did was to take out some pieces of stainless steel to show the druggist the kind of materials we used in our fountains. Then he told him how much the fountain cost. Plainly, the customer was not greatly interested. To me it seemed as if our man was talking too much about us, our product and our wishes, and too little about the customer's problems.

The fountain was a short one, set crosswise at the rear end of the store. There was a cigar counter right up front. And I had noticed that the neighborhood was such that sales of cigars would be confined to cheap brands, bringing little profit.

"If I were in your place I would move the fountain to the front of the store where people will see it," I said to him. "You would do a better fountain business and I believe make more money that way, for in this neighborhood your cigar profits must be rather slim."

Right away the druggist declared he didn't want to spend a lot of money for new fixtures. I explained that I was not recommending new fixtures, just a rearrangement of the old ones. Soon he was interested and agreeing with all I said.

Mr. Bissing talked, not about what his fountain would do to benefit the druggist but about what a rearrangement of equipment would do.

He won interest—and eventually the sale.

Be Ready to Skip Any Step

Occasionally you can skip the interest step in the selling formula. When can you skip this step? When you are absolutely sure that your prospect is interested.

For example, a man came in to see me recently and said, "I have to make a series of speeches in the summer and I want to take some public-speaking course." He showed his interest by that remark. Consequently, I could jump right into the conviction part of my talk—could give him facts as evidence that he would be wise to take our course.

Let's take some of our own medicine. Suppose you ask me why you should be interested in what I have just said? My answer is that it will benefit you. If you get your prospect's interest right at the outset by telling how your goods or services will benefit him, you have a chance to make a sale. If you skip the interest step you have a much poorer chance—probably no chance at all.

Therefore it is not too much to say that if you skip this step, you rarely make the sale.

You don't have to tell me that in this chapter I have repeated the same thing over and over. I have done it deliberately, in the hope that by iteration and reiteration I can drive the point home.

I ask every person who reads this book to take this pledge: *"On my honor, I pledge myself that I shall never again present the body of my sales talk until I am sure I have the prospect's interest."*

Arouse Interest Deliberately

Don't just "take a chance" that you will remember to get your prospect interested. Don't assume that your prospect is interested. Always take it for granted that he isn't—until you have evidence to the contrary. Before you call on any prospect, ask yourself, "How will my goods benefit this particular man?" Determine how they will be of service to him—then get in your mind what you are going to say about this benefit before you ever walk into the presence of your prospect.

Keep on doing it consciously until it becomes habitual.

Once your subconscious mind has taken over the job of reminding you to arouse interest in every prospect, you are at last in a fair way to becoming a real salesman.

CHAPTER EIGHT

Some Additional Rules
for Getting Interest

The ideal of service is the basis of all worthy enterprise.
—Principles of Rotary, 1905.

The Salesman Who Serves Sells

Rule 1: Don't leave the interest step to chance. Don't walk in on your prospect and hope you will think of a good interest getter. Plan it before you walk in.

Rule 2: Ask questions. Keep on asking them all the way through the first three steps of the selling process. Don't stop asking them until you come to the desire step of your sales talk.

Salesmen say, "Many a man has been jailed for making a statement, but they cannot arrest you for asking a question."

Voltaire said, "Judge of a man by his questions, rather than his answers."

Rule 3: Be sure your interest step really is interesting. It will be if it tells the prospect what your goods or service will do to serve him.

Rule 4: To get a prospect interested in anything you can show or demonstrate, let the prospect see it, feel it, ride in it,

43

drive it, taste it, smell it. When I managed a security-sales force in Maine, we used to hand prospects a sample dividend check and say, "How would you like one of these rolling in every three months?"

Rule 5: Keep talking to your prospect about what he will gain, how he will benefit, how he will be served—and you hold his interest automatically, all the way through the sales talk.

Rule 6: Avoid exaggeration. Baltasar Gracian, writing in 1653, said, "Exaggeration is a branch of lying, and you lose by it the credit of good taste, which is much, and of good sense, which is more." Exaggeration is always dangerous, but at the beginning of a sales talk it is often fatal. Guy P. Gannett once said, "When I was buying bonds for the Augusta Trust Company I often had to turn down bond salesmen. One of my favorite ways was to listen closely until the salesman made some exaggerated statement. I'd call him on it. Then, every time he made a true statement, I'd ask him if that was an exaggeration, too. Once you caught a man, he had no defense—and he'd quickly fade out."

If you don't exaggerate or misstate, you will never get caught.

How do I keep from exaggerating? you may ask.

Here's the answer: (*a*) Know your facts. (*b*) Deliberately understate.

Of Course He Doesn't Want to Buy!

Rule 7: Realize that your prospect does not *want* to buy anything. If he wanted to buy it, he would buy it, without

any help from you. He does not even want the article or
service that you are offering. What he does want is what
the article or service will do for him. Tell him about that
and you will get his interest.

Rule 8: Avoid using an interest getter to which the prospect can say, "I'm not interested." If the salesman says, "I
want to show you a new XYZ lamp," the prospect can say,
"I am not interested." If you say, "I want to show you how
you can cut down your electric-light bills," how can the
prospect truthfully say, "I'm not interested?" (To repeat:
Tell the prospect what *he* will get out of it and he must be
interested.)

Rule 9: Talk conversationally, not oratorically. Be natural,
easy. Talk like one friend to another, not like a political
orator repeating a memorized speech.

Some people stop being human when they start selling.
Ann Ashby told me of a little boy who well illustrated this
point. The boy lived next door to the Ashbys in Montclair,
New Jersey, and was in the habit of popping in and out with
no more formality than a puppy.

One day he embarked on a career of selling. He picked
the Ashbys as his first customers. Instead of dropping in and
telling his story informally, he put on a long face, walked
formally up the walk, rang the bell, walked into the parlor,
sat down, and told a long, vague, lugubrious story about his
product. He stopped being human so that he could become
a salesman.

Be natural, human, unaffected, genuine. It pays.

Rule 10: Be super-sincere always—but double-super-sincere
in this part of your talk. The day of the "I'm here to give you

a free book" salesman is about gone, along with the young man selling magazines to pay his way through college.

Nobody Likes to Take Losses

Rule 11: Get your prospect to think about his loss or disadvantage as a result of not owning the goods or service you are selling. Suppose you are selling dictating machines and you say, "Isn't your secretary sitting around hours a day, either taking your dictation or waiting to get it?"

In other words, you get your prospect thinking about a disadvantage that results because he does not use a dictating machine.

Chauncey M. Depew, head of the New York Central Railroad back in the days when being head of a railroad meant something, said, "I would not sit up all of one night to make a hundred dollars—but I would sit up all of seven nights to keep from losing a hundred dollars."

Rule 12: If you accept the prospect's statement, "I can't do anything for you today," you are giving sure evidence that you are no salesman. Unless the purpose of your call is to do some service for the prospect—and unless you can prove it—don't go at all. Don't let him "do something for you"—you do something for him.

Rule 13: "You must have a pleasant manner, and be able to make a favorable impression in thirty seconds." This is one of the Three Golden Rules of Selling given by Arthur C. Fuller, of Fuller Brush fame. Unfortunately, he does not answer the natural queries, "How do you acquire a pleasant manner? How do you make a favorable impression?"

If you begin talking to the prospect about his needs and how your goods or service will supply this need, you don't have to worry much about your manner. When you talk to a man about himself you usually impress him favorably.

Don't Chisel—Serve!

Rule 14: Don't think about yourself—think about your prospect. Put out of your mind all thoughts of the commission you would like to make; put into your mind thoughts about the service your goods will render the prospect. If you begin thinking about how much money you can make by selling this prospect, it will be written all over your face. The prospect's interests in your goods will die at exactly the time when your interest in yourself begins.

Rule 15: Never say to yourself, "I'm going to tell my prospect how good my goods are—and he'll buy." People do not buy on product superiority alone. Of course they expect what they buy to be superior, but primarily they expect it to render a service, to supply a want. Always be sure you know why people will want to buy what you are selling. If you can't find a reason, get a new job. Vacuum-cleaner salesmen don't sell suction—they sell clean rugs.

Rule 16: Talk to your prospect about his problem, his profits, his advancement, his home, his business, his health, his family. Then you can defy him to be uninterested.

Rule 17: Unless you can sell the prospect something that will serve him, don't even call on him. To paraphrase W. J. Cameron: "A salesman who expects to stay in business can't afford to scalp his prospect, for he can scalp the same man only once."

Never write "Not interested" on a prospect card. Write instead, "I failed to get interest."

Selling Maxims

Your prospect's mind is like a parachute—it doesn't work unless it is open.

You're not in there to fool your prospect into buying, so that you can make a profit; you're there to teach him about your product, so that he will gain from owning it.

Go easy on "I"—hard on "you."

CHAPTER NINE

How to Convince Your Prospect

Don't forget the power of plain facts.
—Winans.

Great Rule 3: *Give your prospect enough facts (and no more) about your product or service to convince him that he is justified in buying.*

If you have been successful in the interest step of your sales talk, you have made the prospect say to himself, "If this thing will do what he says, I'd like to have it." Probably he has added to himself, "But I don't believe it will."

Perhaps you have said to him, "A new refrigerator will save you enough electric energy to pay for the machine in five years—so you really get it for nothing." The prospect says to himself, "I'd buy one if I thought I'd get it for nothing—but I don't." Or the salesman says, "These new electric dishwashers actually wash dishes clean—they take off egg, lamb grease, and the other hard-to-move foods." The prospect thinks, "I don't believe a word of it—but I'd like one if it really would wash dishes clean."

You have told your prospect what it will do for him. Now you must prove that it actually will do it.

You may say, "I sell nuts and bolts to purchasing agents. I don't have to prove that they work. What am I supposed to talk about?"

49

My answer is, "Unless your goods or service, terms, price, advertising, or merchandising service is better in some way than your competitors', then what you need is not better selling but a better company to work for. If you know your facts, you can tell a good story about nuts and bolts but a better one about your engineering service or terms or whatever your best talking point may be."

But I'm a Jobber's Salesman

"You can't mean *me*," say jobber salesmen. "Why, we just go around to the same old people and take orders."

All too true. You just take orders—and yet you wonder why your pay hasn't been increased for ten years!

In selling classes I often ask jobbers' salesmen this question, "Suppose you were calling on a dealer who was about to start in business and he asked you, 'Why should I trade with your company?' What would you answer?" I am usually appalled by the reply. It ordinarily runs like this, "Well, it's a fine company. It's been in business a long time. We offer good service. I'd like to have your account." Vague, windy, bragging general claims. No facts. No reasons.

Yet Bertrand R. Canfield in his book "Salesmanship" quotes a recent survey of buyers' motives that confirms the importance of company prestige. It shows that the qualities of a product entered into a sales transaction to the extent of only 15 per cent; the standing of the seller, good will of the company, reputation for service, and similar factors entered in to the extent of 85 per cent.

So be prepared to tell the story of your company and its service.

"Yes," says the jobber's salesman, "but generally I just call back on the same old dealers."

True, of course. But don't you usually have a deal, a promotion plan, or a sales idea to offer? Don't you have to give your customers facts about your company or about its products, its deals, or its advertising? If so you should learn how to do it correctly. So don't skip this chapter. It applies to you practically every step of the way.

Your Appeal Here Is to the Mind

What do you attempt to do in the conviction part of your talk? You try to convince your prospect that your goods or your service are as good as you claim. You appeal to his mind. You give him facts and evidence and testimonials. What your prospect probably wants is the answer to just two questions:

1. What is it?
2. What will it do for me?

Take one of the greatest selling jobs of all history—the job of selling Ferdinand and Isabella the idea of financing Columbus's voyage to find the short route to India. This selling job took six years.

One reason why it took so long is that Columbus could not give the Spanish king and queen facts that would convince them that the trip was practical. Columbus failed in the conviction step.

So would you or I, no doubt, had we faced the objections he did. The Spanish rulers turned the job of hearing the conviction part of his sales talk over to a council at Salamanca, the great seat of Spanish learning. This unknown mariner had to make his sales talk before a gathering of professors, friars, and dignitaries of the church.

While Columbus argued geography, they refuted his statements by quotations from religious writers and the Scriptures and finally adjourned without taking action—which was about equivalent to a "not interested" answer.

Columbus had aroused the cupidity of Ferdinand and the zeal of Isabella. They wanted new lands added to their domain. Desire existed. But they were not convinced—not until almost six years later.

Maybe You're Not So Good As You Think

I never yet saw an experienced salesman who suffered from an inferiority complex with respect to the conviction part of his sales talk.

"I may slip on interest and desire," he says, "but I can surely give them the facts." And he does! His talk usually has all the dullness of the encyclopedia with little of its dignity, and differs from the encyclopedia in that the facts are often wrong!

Does this statement seem unduly pessimistic and cynical? Not if you have, for eighteen years, made ten thousand calls with a thousand salesmen, yawned at the dullness of their talks, and flinched at the wildness of their misstatements.

Most salesmen act as though they considered the conviction part—the body of their sales talk—the most important part. It isn't. It probably ranks in importance fourth out of a possible five.

The conviction part of your sales talk is the defensive part. If you do not present the facts, you may not get the sale.

Equally, however, you may present *all* the facts and still not make the sale.

You might, for example, be a salesman for a crutch company and sell the best crutch in the world; you might give me enough facts to convince me that it *is* the best crutch; but I wouldn't buy. I don't want a crutch!

People don't buy an article on merit alone—they don't buy it because it is best. They buy it because it will serve them.

They don't buy washing machines—they buy freedom from backache. You might list the mechanical advantages of your washing machine for days without making a sale.

People don't buy dictating machines—they buy more working time for their stenographers. What does a man care about the motor or the cutting needle in his dictating machine? He assumes the excellence of the product. What he wants to know is, Will it be convenient for him to use and will it enable his secretary to get out more work?

Convince Him—Don't Asphyxiate Him!

Here are some rules for the conviction part of your sales talk.

Rule 1. Don't drag out this part of your sales talk. Don't give any more dull facts than you need to. Try to make it interesting. Get to the point.

Salesmen tend to substitute talking for thinking.

Another advantage of thinking more and talking less is that it promotes truthful representations. I suspect that some salesmen, after they finish a windy interview, ask themselves sadly, "I wonder what I promised?"

Shakespeare might well have been talking about a sales-

man when in Romeo and Juliet, he said, "A gentleman loves
to hear himself talk, and will speak more in a minute than he
will stand to in a month."

How Long Should It Be?

How long should the conviction part of your talk be?
Long enough to convince your prospect—and no longer.

You Can Usually Guess When to Stop

"If you don't strike oil in two minutes," quotes Albert
Beveridge, "stop boring."

"How am I going to know when to end the conviction part
of my sales talk?" you ask.

Usually you will feel it for yourself.

Don Marquis once wrote, using the editorial "we": "We
were at a dinner the other evening, and we were called on to
say a few words. It suddenly occurred to us, after we had
made certain dull and inept remarks, that we really didn't
have a thing to say, and so we sat down." That's the way
salesmen usually find out when to stop.

The way to find out if you are boring the prospect is to
watch him closely. If he looks out of the window or shuffles
his feet—you have talked too long.

Joseph E. Rogers was quoted as follows in *Printers' Ink:*
"The two great things a salesman should learn is when to talk
and when not to talk—and the greatest of these is when not
to talk. More orders are lost through too much conversation
than from a lack of it." In other words, if in doubt as to
whether or not your prospect is convinced, stop.

Maybe you can't do as many insurance salesmen do, completely hurdle the conviction step of the sale; but you can waste less time in the conviction part of your sales talk than the average salesman does. In talking of the conviction part I mean to include, naturally, the demonstration part of your sales talk. If you sell an article that you can demonstrate, the same general rules apply. The manufacturer will tell you *how* to demonstrate—my part is to tell you not to use too many words in doing it.

Rule 2: Try to locate the key issue and confine your talk largely to that.

If the prospect for a car is primarily interested in gasoline economy, talk chiefly about that. Why worry about appearance, if that does not interest him?

Realsilk salesmen are instructed to locate the prospect's objections to ordinary stockings and then to point out how the makers of Realsilk stockings have overcome that weakness.

Realsilk salesmen locate the key issue for their conviction talk by asking, "At what point do you have the greatest trouble with your stockings? Where do you normally wear out your socks, Mr. Jones? Ever have any trouble with the toes?"

Leonard Lyons ran this item in his column, "The Lyons Den": "Joseph M. Proskauer, the former Supreme Court Justice, . . . subscribes to the London *Times*. . . . Not that he doesn't feel that the N. Y. newspapers supply sufficient news coverage. It's just that he believes that the London *Times* has the finest crossword puzzles in the world."

In other words, if you were trying to sell Judge Proskauer a newspaper you wouldn't talk to him about news coverage; you would talk to him about his key issue, crossword puzzles.

How Much Do You Know?

Rule 3: Know one hundred times as much about the article you are selling as you use in your sales talk. This gives your talk a tone of authority that can be achieved in no other way.

It is astonishing to find how little the average salesman knows about the articles he is selling.

While instructing a sales class in Spokane in the autumn of 1940, I asked a coal salesman to give me the talk he used in selling coal.

He replied, "Well, it's mighty good coal."

"Anything else?" I asked.

"Well, it gives a lot of heat."

"How much?" He didn't know.

"Anything else?"

"It leaves only a little ash."

"How much?" He didn't know.

Finally, annoyed by my badgering, he said, "What *is* there to know about coal?"

What is there to know about coal! I had the matter looked up when I returned to New York. The New York Public Library contains 3,553 books on coal—and more than that number of pamphlets. It has ninety-eight books on furnaces —not all kinds of furnaces, just domestic house-heating furnaces!

What is there to know about coal, indeed!

Lloyd George said, "The surest road to inspiration is preparation."

The magazine *Your Life* quoted Walter Hoving, then president of Lord and Taylor, as follows:

"Although I had taken several courses in college on the appreciation of art and painting, I was so lacking in real knowledge of the subject—which you can readily see is very important in merchandising—that I went for four years to the Metropolitan Museum of Art two nights a week, taking courses in period furniture, old silver, rugs, color, painting, and textile design." He took the trouble to know many hundred times as much about his product as he would ever use in a sales talk. Perhaps that is one reason why he became the youngest department-store president in New York.

"Men give me some credit for genius," said Alexander Hamilton. "All the genius I have lies in this: When I have a subject in hand, I study it profoundly. I study it in all its bearings. My mind becomes pervaded with it. Then the efforts that I make are what people are pleased to call the fruits of genius. It is the fruit of labor and thought."

Surely it will pay you to know what you are talking about.

Rule 4: If you are selling a new article or one that is new to the prospect, try to find out by questions whether he is in the habit of buying something similar. Vacuum cleaners were relatively easy to sell because women had used carpet sweepers. Television sets should be easy to sell because people are in the habit of reaching up into the air with their radio equipment and bringing music, news, and talks down into their homes. What's more reasonable, they will think, than to reach up and pull down motion pictures?

Don't Be Afraid to Repeat

Rule 5: One way to get people to believe what you say is to repeat it again and again. People tend to believe anything

they are told often enough. Apologetically I quote that death-
less—and overworked—statement to Mr. Dooley, "I'll belave
anything at all, if you'll only tell it to me often enough." But
remember, always try to repeat in different words and from
a new angle.

Rule 6: Do not feel that you *always* have to convince your
prospect. Many times you may skip this step entirely.

This is especially true in retail selling, and in some whole-
saling; also in selling some forms of intangibles, insurance
for example. The insurance salesman spends little time telling the merits of his wares—his appeal is usually made
largely to the emotions.

Rule 7: Be sure the prospect knows what you are trying to
sell him.

Does this seem an unnecessary rule? I wish it were! I made
calls with many investment-trust salesmen who neglected to
tell the prospect what it was they were trying to sell. We made
it a rule, therefore, that salesmen must, in the beginning of
the talk, tell the prospect that they were offering an investment trust—and then explain what an investment trust is.

While I was with Henry L. Doherty and Company, a client
of the house called up our New York office from Connecticut
and said, "Your salesman, R. F. D. Lemon, came by my place
yesterday and sold me something and . . . er . . . would
you mind looking up your records and telling me what it
was I bought?"

We're not all R. F. D. Lemons (he was one of the most
powerful salesmen of my long acquaintance). Neither is his
kind of selling always the sort that holds prospects.

So be sure your prospect knows what you are trying to sell

him. I'd blush to write such a rule—if I did not know from my own experience that so many salesmen ignore it entirely.

Don't Be Vague

Rule 8: Be specific. That is, be definite and explicit. Remember, "One hard fact may outweigh all logic and rhetoric."

State facts, not claims. A *Printers' Ink* survey showed that solicitations phrased entirely in generalizations, instead of specific facts, were regarded as the next to worst fault of salesmen. (No. 1 was trying to sell without knowing the business.)

Another poll by *Printers' Ink* shows that buyers of advertising space also object to these practices: (*a*) plain boasting; (*b*) broad, meaningless claims; (*c*) knowing all the answers to everything right off the bat; (*d*) too much blue-sky talk; (*e*) wild ideas; (*f*) exaggerated statements; (*g*) talk—without proof; (*h*) vagueness.

Each one of these offends because it breaks the rule, "Be specific."

Don't dismiss this list as the errors of agency solicitors, applicable only to them. How many of them are your errors? Go over them one at a time. Ask yourself, "Am I guilty of this? Am I guilty of that?" For example, you could say, "Our product is used by one of the largest companies in the world." That would be vague and indefinite. If you say, "It is used by A. T. and T.," it is specific.

"The biggest poison in salesmanship," says Paul W. Ivey, "is the poison of indefinite statements." (If instead of "biggest" he had said "most virulent," "most deadly," "most malignant," he would have been more consistent.)

Many salesmen are as vague as the Yankee who wanted to

compliment the food his host served and said, "It's pretty good—what there is of it; not but that there's enough of it—such as it is!"

Why do salesmen tend to be vague and general in their remarks? Because it's easier. Tom Falvey tells of a salesman out in Ohio who, when asked how much in assets Cities Service had, answered, "I don't know, but they've got a lot."

He hadn't bothered to learn the exact figure, so he gave vent to a picturesque generality.

I went into Altman's once to buy some extra-heavy bath towels. The clerk showed me some that were almost twice as expensive as the next group. So I asked, "Why are these better?" The clerk replied, "Because they cost more." Well, that was specific enough, but hardly the answer. So I asked for the buyer, who gave me a half-dozen reasons why the high-priced towels were superior. I bought them, and they *were* superior—I'm using them yet.

Realsilk Salesmen Use Figures

Realsilk salesmen might say, "Our stockings wear well—wear better than other stockings." This would be a weak claim. Instead, they are taught to be specific—to say: "The Pittsburgh Testing Laboratory made a test for us. They tested 100 Realsilk stockings against 100 leading nationally advertised brands. The people who bought those stockings were instructed to ask for 'the best-wearing chiffon.' Realsilk averaged 250 hours of wear per stocking against 124 hours for the other stockings. Realsilk average hours of wear exceeded other brands by 101 per cent, and the average cost per hundred hours of wear for Realsilk was 60 cents against

$1.02 for competitive brands. It costs 41 per cent less to wear Realsilk."

If this book taught you nothing except to be specific, it would be worth ten times what you paid for it.

Be exact. Be specific. Give facts, not guesses. Don't disguise your ignorance by using broad generalities. Buckle down and learn the facts about your product. Then you can practically eliminate from your vocabulary loose generalities such as "high-grade" and "best quality."

Learn the facts. State the facts. *Be specific.*

Paint "Word Pictures"

Rule 9: Be concrete.

Probably, unless you are a most unusual salesman, you don't know just exactly what the word "concreteness" means. Stop right now and see if you can give a definition of it.

John Dolman, Jr., in his excellent "Handbook for Public Speaking," says, "A thing is concrete in proportion . . . as it creates a picture in the mind's eye, or a sound in the mind's ear or a sensation of touch, taste, or smell."

You can say, "This frame is strong," and your statement is not concrete. But say instead, "You can balance this frame on a beam, load a ton of sandbags on each end, sight down the top, and see that it has not even bent—much less buckled." This brings a picture to your mind's eye—a picture of yourself squinting down the frame, to see if it has bent.

Concreteness is important in this part of your sales talk, but even more important in arousing desire. So you will hear more of it as you read on.

Rule 10: Be clear. Unless your prospect understands just exactly what you are talking about, you're better off not to talk.

Your prospect buys not because of what you say but because of what he understands and believes of what you say. Keep asking yourself, "Is he following me? Is he understanding me? Is he believing me?"

When I was selling preferred stock for the Central Maine Power Company I got out a circular with a highly colored map on the back. The salesmen took delight in "selling from the map," as they called it. One day I went out with a salesman named Campbell. Mr. Campbell made a sales talk on the preferred stock, using the map as an exhibit. When he was about half way through his canvass for the preferred stock, his prospect said, "No, I don't think I want to buy a map today."

That salesman, who was an exceptionally effective one as a rule, had failed to make his prospect understand what he was offering.

"I make it a rule to believe only what I understand," wrote Disraeli. So do most people.

How can you be clear? Well, here are a few suggestions.

(a) Have your subject clearly in your own mind. About half the fuzzy selling in this country today is due to fuzzy thinking.

One night, when I was teaching a public-speaking class, I made this criticism of a speech: "It isn't exactly clear to me."

The speaker replied, "Well, I'm not surprised. It isn't exactly clear to me, either."

After that, I wasn't surprised, either.

Albert J. Beveridge says, "Make every sentence so plain

that the dullest or most uninformed person cannot fail to understand the meaning of what is said."

(b) Use short, familiar words. Never use a long word when a short one will do equally well.

(c) Don't talk too fast.

(d) Don't expect customers to understand the jargon of your trade or profession or business.

Here's an example: One afternoon Mark Twain, who lost more than one hard-earned fortune by investing it in harebrained schemes described to him in glittering terms, observed a tall, spare man, with kindly blue eyes and eager face, coming up the path with a strange contraption under his arm. Yes, it was an invention, and the man explained it to the humorist, who listened politely but said he had been burned too often.

"But I'm not asking you to invest a fortune," exclaimed the man. "You can have as large a share as you want for $500." Mark Twain shook his head; the invention didn't make sense. The tall, stooped figure started away.

"What did you say your name was?" the author called after him.

"Bell," replied the inventor a little sadly, "Alexander Graham Bell."   —VANSANT CORYELL in *The Christian Science Monitor.*

The chances are the inventor had failed to make clear what his contraption was or what it would do.

Insurance salesmen who have called on me have been bad offenders in this respect. I rarely know what they are talking about.

(e) Try to illustrate the points you make by drawing rough sketches or diagrams.

Experiments show that people remember some of what they hear, more of what they see, and still more of what they both see and hear. By using a pad and pencil, your prospect will both see and hear what you are saying. (Avoid, however, making meaningless drawings or putting down nonsensical figures. Some salesmen, with a pad and pencil in their hands, cover the paper with mere scribbling, or "doodles." This does no good and may even distract the prospect's attention. Put down only such figures or such diagrams as help your prospect to understand and believe your story.)

Why Talk, Unless You Are Understood?

I remember once, when we were selling power-company securities, that Joe Martin, one of our salesmen, announced in a sales meeting, "I'm going to take a night course in electricity."

To this his sales manager replied, "If you do, I'll fire you. All you'd get out of it would be some more big words—and your customers don't know what you're talking about now."

Quintilian said, "Not that language may be understood but that it cannot be misunderstood."

The Birds Eye people were trying to make clear to housewives how much they were putting into their packages of frozen food. They could have said of lima beans, for example, "This package contains eleven ounces or two cupfuls." Instead, they instructed their clerks to say, "It serves four." This was clear to the housewife.

Rule 11: Manage the interview—don't let your prospect manage it. If he tries to carry the conversation off the track, show only mild interest in the unrelated and immaterial subject. As soon as you can, say, "Let's see, what were we talking about?" and then get back on your sales talk.

Rule 12: Speak good English.

How?

It's easy enough—by studying English all your life. Buy any one of a dozen good books on correct English (preferably pocket size) and go to work. Then buy another and another. Never stop as long as you live.

Is it important? Yes, vitally so. The salesman who habitually uses bad English is offensive to a considerable number of people. They will not enjoy talking with him. In some cases, this will be true of people who do not speak correctly themselves.

Professor Austin Phelps said, "The common people know good English when they hear it; they understand it. Men crave it who never use it."

Rule 13: "You must have enthusiasm for the product you are selling," says Arthur C. Fuller. He continues, "If you have this, the prospect will feel and respond to it. Enthusiasm is the mysterious electric current that flows from seller to buyer. It can't be seen any more than electricity can, but it can be felt."

Have I mentioned enthusiasm before? I have. And I expect to mention it again. It is one quality that must appear in every step of the sales talk.

Be warned by this statement of A. J. Balfour's: "It is unfortunate, considering that enthusiasm moves the world, that so few enthusiasts can be trusted to speak the truth."

Or, translating it into salesmen's talk, "Don't let your enthusiasm betray you into exaggeration—or worse!"

If You Have to Eat Soap—Eat Soap!

Rule 14: Jounce your prospect once in a while. Don't let your talk get in a rut. Wake him up.

How? Well, one example is the man who was peddling soap who used to ask the housewife if the soap she was using was pure enough to eat. Then, to jounce her a bit, he would put a piece of his soap in his mouth and solemnly chew it.

An accident insurance salesman used to stop in the middle of his talk, whip out a picture of an automobile wreck, point to one of the wrecked cars, and say, "The driver of that car was in the hospital two years after that accident. His family went on relief—because he had no accident insurance." Zenn Kaufman, for use in his Showmanship speech, has a number of hammers made of balsa wood. They are painted to look as though they weighed ten pounds each—actually they are so light they will almost float in air. In the middle of his speech, without warning, he throws a handful of these hammers into his audience. This stunt is a real jouncer.

Rule 15: A good way to test interest is to stop now and then, look the prospect right in the eye, and say, "Have I made it clear?" If you feel that you have lost the prospect's interest, stop in the middle of a sentence and pause. The prospect will come back to attention—usually with a healthy start.

Rule 16: Talk in a convincing tone, use convincing movements and gestures. Norvall Hawkins pointed out that a prospect may be suspicious of your words, no matter how fair, because he knows that words can conceal ideas and feelings and motives. The prospect knows, however, that a sincere tone of voice and sincere motions can hardly be counterfeited.

How can you be sure that your tones and gestures are sincere and convincing? You know the answer, of course—don't sell anything that you don't believe in. If you can't recommend it sincerely, don't sell it. If you sell something you don't

believe in, you are only a little better than a sneak thief—
and you will not last long at selling.

Sell the Gadgets Too

Rule 17: Don't pin all your faith on one or two major selling points of your product or service. Use secondary points
as well.

One of the first security sales I ever made was to a woman
who lived north of Augusta, Maine. She bought so easily that
after I got the money, I asked her what she liked particularly
about the stock.

Her answer was, "The money comes to me every three
months by check." That minor selling point was the major
point in her case. If I had left it out, I might have missed the
sale. She assumed the safety of principal and the certainty
of income and the other major points—but she didn't like to
bother to go to Augusta to cash bond coupons.

F. W. Potter, writing in *The Aetna-izer*, said, "Sell the
gadgets"—then he supported his command with this example.

I talked with the leading salesman of a certain make of automobile
and asked him concerning his sales technique. He said—"It's the
little things about the car that help the sale. The other day a man
and his wife came into the show room. I showed them, among other
things, the engine of the model they were interested in. The wife
remarked, "All motors look alike." I then changed my tactics and
said, "I wish you would look inside the car. You will notice we
put a vanity case on each side of the rear seat, with a handy cigarette
lighter beside it." Immediately the wife started to show interest.
In a few minutes they decided to buy.

The motors all looked alike, but the vanity case was different!

Don't Get Bored with Your Own Sales Arguments

Rule 18: Don't discard selling points, examples, or testimonials, just because *you* are tired of them.

I went out once with a salesman and heard him flounder through some important points with the use of twice as many words as necessary. So I said to him, "Why don't you say that the way you used to?"

He answered, "Because I am tired of it."

My reply, naturally enough, was, "Yes, but your client never heard it before."

Try to get a one best way to present a point—then don't change it until you have used it once on every prospect.

Do you want to know how to keep from getting bored with saying it over and over the same way? I'll give you an example of a man who didn't get tired. Back in 1902, I interviewed Joseph Jefferson, then perhaps the most distinguished actor in America, who was playing "Rip Van Winkle" in the Vendome Theatre in Nashville. He had played "Rip Van Winkle" thousands of times. So I asked him, "Don't you get tired of playing the same part over and over?"

He smiled when he replied, "Lots of people ask me that. And it is true, I used to get bored with the repetition. One day I faced the issue. I said to myself, 'Joe Jefferson, are you playing that part for your own amusement—or for the amusement of those people down front?' As soon as I forgot myself and got to thinking of my audience I was never bored again by that or any other part."

So if you are bored by saying your sales talk the one right way, just remind yourself, "I am here to convince my prospect. He has not heard this done right before—but he's going to *now*." Then tell it to him in the one best way.

Don't Skip Important Points

Rule 19: Don't *forget* any of your selling points, either.

I remember that once we were offering a security that had just seven points we wanted presented. I called for nearly a week with different salesmen. I noted that none of them seemed to be telling the whole story, which could be told completely in ten or twelve minutes. So I began checking to see if salesmen were presenting all seven points. I never found even one who did—unless I called his attention to it in advance. Finally, we made lists of the seven points, on 3 by 5 cards, and required salesmen to keep referring to this, in order to be sure they were presenting the seven important points.

The Brunswick-Balke-Collender Company supply their salesmen with "cue cards" (vest-pocket size) on which are listed the selling points they want used. They have different cards for different campaigns and plans.

Rule 20: Prove some of the things you say, but don't bother to prove everything. People take a lot on faith. They believe a lot of things they don't understand. "He that will believe only what he can fully comprehend," said Colton, "must have a very long head, or a very short creed."

Rule 21: Let your customer feel he is deciding for himself.

Snow says, "The wise salesman is the one who can make his customers believe that their judgment is not influenced to any extent by what the salesman says."

Thus: "Mr. Blank, I've given you the facts—you make the decision."

Rule 22: Have places in your talk where you replace words with *action*. Stop talking entirely, and show an exhibit, draw a diagram, or do a little arithmetic.

Rule 23: Don't talk all the time, especially when you are demonstrating.

Plutarch tells the story of Demaratus, who, upon being asked in a certain assembly whether he held his tongue because he was a fool or for want of words, replied, "A fool cannot hold his tongue."

Some salesmen talk as though they were in constant fear that the prospect would interrupt! Let him, *let him!*

The early part of a sales talk should usually contain more questions than statements. Get your prospect's story first. Don't try to cut him short—really *listen* to him. Most salesmen ought to take a course in listening.

It is not enough that you ask questions and then sit back and think about something else. You must listen, attentively and with interest. "Few human beings," said Jack Woodford in "Strangers in Love," "are proof against the flattery of rapt attention."

See that your attention is "rapt"—that you listen as though you enjoyed it.

It takes a great salesman to be a good listener.

Real estate salesmen are among the worst of the nonstop talkers. One of them is showing you through a residence. "This is the bathroom." (You thought it was the garage.) "This is the kitchen." (Curiously, you had already suspected it.) "Tile floor." (You'd picked it for an oriental rug.) And so through the house, out into the street, and out of the sale.

"Much talk, much foolishness," says the Talmud—which is a good aphorism for salesmen to remember.

Let the Prospect Sell Himself

John Batdorff of Cleveland told me this story about himself:

I've been in the real estate business off and on for eighteen years. A little over a month ago I read in a book the rule: "Don't try to do all the talking yourself—let your prospect do his share." So I tried it. I was showing an expensive house to a wealthy man. I unlocked the front door, said, "Well, here it is," and ushered him in. I stayed outside. He came out in a half hour or so and said, "I sort of like it. I'd like to show it to my wife." Did I offer to show it? I did not. I handed him the key. In an hour he was at the office, all smiles. "Well," he said, "I sold it to my wife." *He* sold it, but I got the commission.

Try it yourself.

One of the great selling delusions is: "The more talk, the more sales." Don't fall a victim to this fallacy.

Kenneth Gruesbeck tells this little story in a magazine article:

"Well, did you buy the washing machine?" asked her husband.

"No, I did not," answered his wife decisively. "The salesman talked so much I didn't get a chance to look at it, so I just walked out on him."

This story, with the product changed, is an actual fact.

If this salesman had asked one or two questions to discover his prospect's state of mind, he would have taken her direct to the appliance and let her see it and use it herself. That was all this particular woman needed. She would have bought if she had been given a chance.

Rule 24: Test your prospect's attention every little while. How? Ask a question.

A prospect can look you right in the eye, say Yes now and then, nod his head repeatedly—and not take in one word you are saying!

A question will always bring his attention back.

What If Your Prospect Wriggles?

Rule 25: Suppose your prospect takes no pains to hide his lack of interest. He wriggles in his chair, shuffles his feet, looks out of the window. What should you do?

Ask yourself first why he lacks interest. Possibly you are interfering with a golf date, maybe you are keeping him away from some rush job, maybe it's just indigestion.

If you suspect his lack of interest is due to some such cause as this, say, "Mr. Blank, have I come in at a bad time— am I interfering with some important engagement?" He will doubtless tell you. Then you can, if it seems wise, make a definite appointment for a later date and withdraw.

If, on the other hand, it develops that he has no reason to wriggle except that he is bored with your sales talk, then ask him some questions designed to learn why he isn't interested. You are likely to find out that he is not interested because you have left him out of the picture. You are saying, "Our company is the largest of its kind in the world, our company this, our president that, our sales manager something else"—

and never a word about what the product will do to serve or benefit the prospect.

So when the prospect is just plain bored, start talking about *him,* put on more steam, show more sincerity and enthusiasm, ask questions—and watch the magic transformation.

Nail Down Your Points

Rule 26: Nail down the important points as you make them. Suppose you have been giving a prospect your reasons for believing that your tire is a safe tire; you can say, "When you consider these facts, you agree with me, don't you, that this is a safe tire?"

Or suppose you are selling a man an educational insurance policy; you might say, after you have done some computing, "Well, these figures indicate, don't they, Mr. Blank, that you ought to have about $25,000 worth of education insurance?"

In other words, after you make each important point, ask your prospect a question about that point which he must answer with Yes. Gradually you are building up your case. If the prospect has agreed, as he has been carried through the sales talk, that your product is the only one that exactly fits his wants, it becomes quite difficult for him to say No when you ask the deciding question.

The National Cash Register Company used to recommend that its men list the points they wanted to cover on a large writing pad. Their instructions for nailing down these points follow:

As each important thing is covered, question the merchant in order to find out if he understands you. For example, "I believe you will agree with me, Mr. Blank, that this is a better way of handling this transaction than your present method, won't you?" If he is not convinced, explain to his satisfaction before going further. When he is thoroughly convinced, check off the point covered on the large writing pad. You will then know that the merchant is following you and is convinced as far as you have gone.

Be Alive, Act Alive, Talk Alive

Rule 27: Be vocally animate. Don't talk in a monotone—stress important syllables and words. Don't talk always in the same pitch—drop to a lower pitch to underline some important thought. Another way of calling attention to important points is to speak the important words more slowly. Still another is to set off the important words with pauses before and after.

Practice all these devices for giving yourself vocal animation, but especially drill yourself to use pauses. Don't just run on. Pause once in awhile, for dramatic effect.

Evidence of the effectiveness of pauses is given by this historical example from "Better English":

When Edmund Burke was delivering his famous speech against Warren Hastings, he suddenly stopped in the middle of an idea. Slowly and impressively he raised his hand and pointed his index finger straight at Mr. Hastings. There he stood, for almost a minute, with that dramatic pointing finger while the audience almost held its breath. Then he went on.

After the speech one of the opposing advocates came up to him and said, "Mr. Burke, that was one of the most effective pauses I have ever seen. We simply held our breaths, wondering what you were going to say next."

"That," responded Mr. Burke with his Irish twinkle, "is exactly the way I was feeling."

Maxims

It takes a good salesman to be a good listener.

The first test of a salesman's English is: Do people *understand* it?

Think faster than your prospect thinks, but don't *talk* faster than he thinks.

Few salesmen ever miss a good opportunity to talk, but lots of them miss what Winston Churchill called "a very fine opportunity for keeping quiet."

Never say, "To make a long story short." It's probably too late.

No one objects to how much you say, if you say it in a few words.

When you are making a sales talk, think only of two things —your goods and how they will serve the prospect.

"The salesman talks most who has the least to say."— PRYOR (as amended).

"No wild beast is more to be dreaded than a communicative salesman—with nothing to communicate."—SWIFT (brought up to date).

Stop talking when you are through, or slightly before.

Lots of salesmen cannot keep from talking too much, even at the risk of losing the sale.

You don't have to prove every statement you make, but be sure to prove one now and then just in case!

Don't sell the product, sell results.

CHAPTER TEN

How to Build a Sales Talk

Let thy speech be short, comprehending, much in few words.
—SHAKESPEARE.

How do you build the conviction part of your sales talk? Needless to say, it depends on an infinite number of factors. Here are some good general rules that have worked for years for men under my direction.

1. Write down on separate pieces of paper every single selling point that you can think of. Just a word or two to identify it, like "safety of principle," "wearing qualities of motor," "efficient service available."

2. Arrange your selling points in logical order.

3. Pick out some examples, statistics, or testimonials that tend to support or prove your claims for your product.

(Complete directions for writing the conviction part of your sales talk will be found in the next chapter.)

How You Can Prove That Your Claims Are True

*Ah! what avails the classic bent
And what the cultured word
Against the undoctored incident
That actually occurred?*
—KIPLING.

How can you convince your prospect that the claims you make about your products are true?

One of the best ways is with examples.

So pack the conviction part of your talk with "examples"— with verbal testimonials. For instance:

"A dictating machine will save your secretary an hour or more each day. John Smith, down at 270 Smith Street, put in dictating equipment a year ago—and within a week could let a stenographer go and still keep up with his dictating. He saved over $2,000 a year."

Or another example: "These cars save their owners money on repair bills. We sold one three years ago to John Jones. He has driven it over 100,000 miles. He tells me that repairs have cost him under $100 in three years."

The smart salesman is always on the lookout for striking examples. If he is exceptionally smart he will write them down and file them.

Don't pass this over as "just another rule." Try it—and keep on trying. Get examples, learn to tell them well, then keep on telling them.

They liven up a sales talk. They are convincing. Don't just make claims—give evidence that the claims are true.

"Any fact is better established," says Emmons, "by two or three good testimonials than by a thousand arguments."

Every time you make a general statement in your talk, try to back it up with an example. For instance, "This newspaper pulls." That's just a claim. Then you back it up with some evidence. "Brown and Smith ran an advertisement Friday, two columns by ten inches, and sold over $1,000 worth of merchandise."

Another example. "This car is fast." ("That's what you think," says the prospect.) "I never crowded one to see what it would do, but I heard Jim Jones say that he'd had his up above ninety miles an hour." (This statement is evidence—and is convincing.)

Use examples. If you learn nothing else out of this book but this point, you will bless me all your selling life.

What made Dale Carnegie's "How to Win Friends and Influence People" sell over three million copies? Thirty-seven good rules and hundreds of examples that served as evidence that the rules worked.

What makes a speech interesting—if it is? Examples! No matter how dull a speech is, if the speaker says "For example," your hopes revive. Maybe it isn't going to be so dull after all.

Examples make both speeches and sales talks. Use plenty.

Try All These Kinds of Examples

Richard C. Borden, in his book "Public Speaking as Listeners Like It" (which every salesman should own, even if he never expects to make a speech in his life), gives some excellent suggestions as to the kinds of examples which interest people. We paraphrase from his book:

1. Use "instances" in story form. (But be sure they are *true* stories—fiction is worthless in selling. Some security salesmen are in jail today because they didn't observe this simple rule: "Tell the exact and complete truth.")

Let me give you an example of an example in story form: "The John C. Smith Company was always behind with its bookkeeping. Its force worked nights and holidays, but they couldn't catch up. Bills went out late. Reports were six weeks behind. . . ." But why go on!

2. Next consider examples about celebrities.

Do you want some examples? You have already had several in this book. One was Ben Franklin and the advertisement for wagons.

Weyerhaeuser salesmen use this example. They ask: "Did you know that it is practically impossible to wear out a Douglas fir wood gutter? Did you know that a Douglas fir gutter costs less than gutters of other materials, lasts longer, and requires less maintenance? For instance, when the White House was remodeled recently, a section of wood gutter was removed that had been in use for 110 years. It was still sound and serviceable, though it had never been painted."

Their example was interesting because it used a name familiar to virtually everyone in the United States, the White House.

3. Examples from history are often effective.

An instance of an example from history follows: "You have to advertise persistently to get results. Look at Columbus. He spent eighteen years selling his idea of a round-the-world trip to India. But he finally discovered something worth many trillion-trillions of dollars—the Americas."

4. Analogies often produce results. Most of you know what an analogy is. For the benefit of the few who don't, Webster's *Collegiate* says it is ". . . a resemblance of relations; agreement between things in some circumstances but not in others."

Analogous cases are effective weapons for salesmen. If you don't consciously use them, you ought to.

Take the point your customer does not admit and show that it is similar in many respects to one he does admit.

A salesman in offering an investment trust might say, "You buy insurance, don't you? Well, an insurance company is just an investment trust, with one added feature."

Or suppose you were selling an electric dishwashing machine, you might give this analogous case: "How do they dig away dirt in a placer mine? By shooting water against it. Well, in this dishwasher . . ."

Make Your Figures Move

Another way to support your claims is with statistics. When you use figures try to dramatize them. Examples: "He's driven that car over 400,000 miles—as far as from here to the moon, and beyond." "As tall as the Empire State Building." "If laid end to end, would circle the globe."

Don't just give figures—make them live!

Another way to support your claims is with statements from authorities or from satisfied users.

If you quote authorities be sure

(a) That they are known to the prospect as authorities. For example, if you were selling a book to coal miners and you could truthfully state, "John L. Lewis says that every coal miner should read this book," you would be quoting a recognized authority.

(b) Or that if they are not known to the prospect, you "qualify them"—that is, you give reasons why their opinion is of value. For instance, when I am qualifying myself as a speaker in sales training, I say, "I was a sales manager for nineteen years. In that time I trained 72,000 men and women to sell."

If you support your claims with statements by satisfied users, follow the two rules above and add a third rule, to wit: "Have plenty." In selling the Dale Carnegie Course in Effective Speaking we hand the prospect a booklet and say to him, "Here are the names and addresses of 1,375 people who have taken the course and are satisfied with it. Call one of them or a score of them and ask them if we delivered everything we promised." The prospect is impressed with the large numbers of satisfied users.

Use exhibits. For example: "These dictating machine records last—here's one which has been shaved xy times." "This machine does fine tabulating work. Look at this sample page and note the fine alignment." "Let me show you why these tires stand up. Here's a cross section of one of them. Note . . ."

The average man is said to remember one tenth of what he hears, three tenths of what he sees, and five tenths of what he both sees and hears.

What if your company does not supply you with anything to demonstrate? An old salesman once said, "Tell me anything you want me to sell, then give me ten minutes to think and a half hour to browse around a five-and-ten, and I'll turn up with a demonstration and something to do it with.

Try hard to find something you can show your prospect, something he can look at, handle, feel, smell of, maybe taste. A visual example tends to liven up your talk—and to convince your prospect.

A recent quiz on the methods of 213 sales managers indicated that a dramatized presentation—an appeal to both eyes and ears—was eight times as effective as an oral message in getting over a sales point.

The Secret of Making Examples Interesting

Here are a few added suggestions of my own:

1. Make your example specific. (Don't say, "Many people have bought lots in this development." Say, "John Smith, owner of the *News*, just bought a lot at the corner of Main and X Street in our subdivision. Two weeks ago we sold one to . . .")

2. Make your examples concrete—that is, paint a word picture. (If you were selling a world cruise you might say, "You travel in a boat so big that if you put it down in Fifth Avenue with the bow at 42d Street, the stern would be way down by . . .")

3. Which leads up to the next point—don't try to make your example too brief. Use enough words to make it interesting.

4. Make your examples move. Tell a story, have a plot. That would not be clear without an example, so here it is:

The salesman selling a sales course might say, "I know a man who got two raises of pay while he was taking the course." But how much better to put some life in it, thus:

"John Smith of 234 Smith Street, Smithville, who took our sales course in Cleveland, told this story: 'Two weeks before I enrolled, my boss came to me and said, "You are so absolutely rotten I haven't the heart to fire you, but I wish you'd resign." I told the boss I was going to take the course, so he let me stay. The course transformed my life. The boss, who wanted me to resign, gave me two raises in pay while I was taking it. It transformed me from a coward to a man.'"

That is the "before-and-after" testimonial.

Another standard treatment is the "one did and the other didn't" form, for instance:

A salesman in selling speaking courses to women said: "Two girls whom I know were paid workers for a charity organization. They had the same kind of job—received the same pay. An opening developed, a grand promotion with practically double the pay. One of these girls could have it—but which one? They were so nearly equal in every respect that they were asked just one question, 'Can you speak in public?' Only one of the girls could honestly answer Yes. She got the job."

These two examples tell you what I mean by having examples that have a plot—that move.

5. Try to get examples that happened to you or that you know about personally. An example out of a book or a newspaper may be good, but an example within your own experience is vastly better. Why? Because you can tell it better. (I admit this rule can be questioned. I base it on hearing tens of thousands of sales talks and almost as many student speeches. As a rule the personal experience sparkles—the others do not.)

Some More Suggestions for Writing Your Sales Talk

Now to get back to our other suggestions for writing out your sales talk:

1. Write what you want to say about each point.

Be sure that you write each point, when possible, in terms of your prospect's interests. Be sure it is in answer to his unspoken question, "How will this point serve or benefit me?" Not "This is the lightest pencil in the world," but "Because this is the lightest pencil in the world, you can use it all day without getting tired."

2. Now go back and cut out any sales point you don't actually need. Be heartless about it. Probably you can get rid of about half of the points—to the great benefit of your talk.

3. Connect them up so that there are no gaps between them.

4. Ruthlessly cut out about half the words. Sales talks are like rough diamonds in this respect—they are improved by cutting. The brilliance and sparkle of a diamond is achieved by carefully cutting away about half the stone. This cutting increases its value immensely. The same is true of a sales talk. Cut away half the talk and it will be worth twice as much money to you.

Yes, It's a Big Job, But It's Worth It

"Great heavens!" you say. "How long will this take?"

"Hours, days, weeks," is our answer, "if you do it carefully."

Is it worth all that time?

That depends largely, of course, on what you are selling.

If you are selling one article or service—insurance, securities, advertising space, vacuum cleaners, washing machines, dictating machines, correspondence courses—for which you use the same talk day after day, then it is hardly possible for you to put in too much time working on your sales talk.

"When I have done all this work in writing out the conviction part of my sales talk," you ask in accents of undoubted horror, "do you expect me to learn it by heart?"

No, I don't expect you to learn it by heart. You *have* learned it by heart. Or substantially, at least. This is the compensation for all the work you do—you practically memorize the conviction part of your sales talk as a result of working it over and over.

Get It Right—Then Don't Change It

Then should you present it the way you have written it? By all means. Once you have found the one best way of saying it, why say it some weaker way?

One of the best defenses of canned sales talks I ever read was an article in *Sales Management* for May, 1924, by J. R. MacPherson, president, Hooven-Chicago Company. He required his salesmen to write out their canned selling talk three times a day for fifteen days—forty-five times in all—before he would let them try to sell. Mr. MacPherson finished his article with this statement:

Give me the most brilliant salesman you can find. Let him start out with a haphazard sales canvass, based on his own ideas of what facts the customer ought to know. I'll pick up the rankest amateur, require him to write my selling talk forty-five times, and the amateur will outsell the experienced man every time.

I remember training one fellow to sell bank supplies. It was always a mystery to me how he ever broke into the training school. You would never select him as a salesman. No initiative, no imagination, no personality. Nothing! Except the ability to do as he was told.

I remember we told him that he would never be allowed to go into the field as a salesman unless he could recite the selling talk word for word—letter perfect before the entire class. When he recited the talk he was rather hesitant and his voice was very low. We forced him to stand thirty feet away from the listeners and recite the entire sales canvass in a voice we could all hear.

When he was preparing to leave, he came and asked me what I

would do when I landed in the territory if I were in his place. I
thought he was hopeless, but merely to get rid of him I told him
to go to the first county in his territory, call on every bank in the
county one after another, and repeat his sales talk to every bank
purchasing agent in that county before he went to the next county.
He did just that. And he sold every bank in the first county he
worked. His earnings the first month were $600. Before long he ran
his commissions up as high as $1,100 in one month. Do you wonder
that I am strong for set talks in sales work?

Your Own Canned Talk Is Best for You

Why do I like my plan (of having the salesman write his
own sales talk) better than Mr. MacPherson's plan (of having
him learn a talk that somebody else wrote)? For several reasons. One is that it is extremely difficult for a man to memorize
the other man's sales talk. For another thing, unless you write
the talk yourself, it will not be in the words you would naturally use, and hence will sound artificial—unless you are a
born actor, which probably you are not.

"What are you going to do if you sell a line of goods where
it is impracticable to spend much time on any one item?"
you ask.

I can only answer, "Do your best." You will gradually
find the one best way to say the important things—why worry
about the others?

Picture the Prospect as Owning the Product

On the following pages I give you many suggestions for
making the conviction part of your sales talk interesting and

effective. One point, however, is so important that it should
stand out by itself. Here it is:

Keep your prospect in the picture. Talk in terms of his
interests. Picture him as already owning the product. For
example, you could say, "This bond pays 4 per cent." But
suppose you picture the prospect as owning the bond. "When
you own this bond, Mr. Blank, you can go to the bank twice
a year and cut and cash your coupon for $20—$40 each year
on your thousand for twenty years—then your money back in
full." Or suppose you were selling a car, you could say, "This
car does 80 miles an hour easily." Or you could talk in terms
of the prospect's interest and say, "You can step in this car
in front of your office at 5:30 and you can be rolling up your
front driveway at 5:42."

In phrasing your sales talks, assume always that your prospect is going to buy what you offer. Not "This radio has a
lovely tone," but "When we take out your old radio and
install this in your library, you can shut your eyes, sit back,
and listen to symphony orchestras and find it hard to be sure
whether you are at home or in Symphony Hall."

"Shucks," you say, "I sell hacksaw blades. How can you
get romantic telling a purchasing agent about hacksaw
blades?"

Well, workmen *use* them, don't they? I don't know too
much about hacksaws myself, but surely you can say, "When
the men of your company put these blades . . ." I know
that carpenters are as much interested in the feel of a ham-
mer or saw as you are in the feel of a golf club or a split
bamboo rod.

The use of this idea of bringing the prospect into the talk—

of picturing him using the article—will brighten up your sales talk amazingly. James Russell Lowell said:

Not a deed would he do, not a word would he utter
Till he'd weighted its relation to plain bread and butter.

So talk to the prospect about his bread and butter.

CHAPTER ELEVEN

How to Test Your Sales Talk

I never did anything worth doing by accident, nor did any of my inventions come by accident; they came by work.
—THOMAS A. EDISON.

Many salesmen write out the body of their sales talk, but few use it after it is written. They don't use it because it is a poor sales talk, and it is a poor sales talk because they haven't done enough work on it.

Here are some suggestions for writing this part of your sales talk and for testing it after it is written:

First

What to Do before You Write It

Before you write, ask yourself:

A. Have I a real interest in the people to whom I shall make this talk? Am I interested in their problems? Do I even know what these problems are? (Unless you are sincerely interested in your prospect, don't bother to write this sales talk —because you will never need it.)

B. Have I visualized my prospect, so that I can talk *to* him and not *at* him? Is this talk aimed at an average prospect, or at a specific prospect who can use my goods or services?

C. Have I said to myself:

89

1. What is the purpose I wish to achieve in this, the body of my sales talk—what idea am I trying to sell?

The purpose of the conviction part of your sales talk is to convince the prospect that it will be an intelligent move to buy what you are offering. This is the part of your sales talk where you appeal to his brains. As you write each sentence, each word, keep this purpose in mind and keep asking yourself if you are accomplishing it.

2. Have I qualified myself to make this part of my sales talk? In short, have I won the right to make it?

You have no right to take up your prospect's time unless you have a broad knowledge of and great enthusiasm for what you are talking about, and unless you are trying to sell him something that will really benefit him.

3. As I make a point in favor of my product, have I made it in terms of my prospect's interests?

For example, if you are selling a dictating machine, don't say, "This machine will increase the efficiency of your office force," but put it in terms of your prospect's interests. Thus: "When you equip your secretary with a dictating machine, she will have at least one hour more a day to give to her other duties."

4. Have I painted some word pictures in this part of my sales talk as well as later, in the desire step?

It is desirable to tell your prospect what your goods will do *in general*. It is better to tell what they will do for the prospect *specifically*. It is best of all to paint a picture of the prospect's *enjoyment* of these goods. For instance, to continue the dictating machine example, you might say: "When the morning mail is dropped on your desk by your secretary, your natural desire is to answer it immediately.

If you are equipped with a dictating machine you pick up the mouthpiece and start dictating. Should the telephone ring, you merely hang up the mouthpiece, pick up the phone, and carry on your conversation. However, if you are dictating to your secretary and the telephone rings, her time, which is costing you money, is being spent looking at her fingernails while you carry on your conversation."

5. Does this part of my talk answer the probably unspoken question of my prospect, "What will it do for me?"

6. Does this part of my talk have action and incident?

Ask yourself, "What example will tell my story—will be evidence of the truth of my statement?" Put in plenty of examples.

Second

How to Compose Your Talk

Now then, start to write the conviction part of your sales talk. Here are some points you ought to watch:

A. Remember that in this part of your talk you are trying to convince your prospect of the wisdom of buying your goods. You are appealing to his head, his brains.

B. Keep your prospect in the picture. Don't say, "This machine will cut costs," but instead say, "Your machine will save you $10 a month."

C. To repeat—pile up the examples. Make them interesting. Be sure they are relevant—that they tell a story which supports the point you are trying to make.

D. Write each sentence just as you would say it if you were talking to a friend. Ask yourself constantly, "How would I say that?"

92 THE FIVE GREAT RULES OF SELLING

E. Keep both your words and your sentences short and simple.

F. Imagine that your prospect is constantly repeating these two questions:

"Why?"

"What difference does it make to me?"

You say, "Ours is the best." Imagine that your prospect then asks, "Why?"—and tell him.

You say, "Our company is the largest in its line in the United States." Imagine that your prospect then asks "Yes, but what difference does that make to me?"—and tell him.

Third
After You Have Written Your Sales Talk

Check through to see if you are right on these points.

A. As to unity:

1. Does your talk give or imply every fact the prospect ought to know? (You rarely can give all the facts—but you can imply them.)

2. Do you try to make more than one main point? If you try to sell more than one idea, if you ask your prospect to do several things, you're probably wrong. Concentrate on one thing.

B. As to coherence: Do you anywhere interrupt the steady flow of your prospect's thoughts—do you give him a chance to "drop through" or quit? Don't! It may be fatal to your cause. Tie your paragraphs together.

C. As to force:

1. Does your talk go directly to the point, or does it wander and digress? (Don't be a human grasshopper!)

2. How will each word, phrase, and sentence impress the prospect? Will it move him along in the direction you want him to go? (Read each sentence aloud. Then ask yourself: How will that sound to my prospect? How will he react to it?)

3. Does your talk lead to a climax of thought and feeling that causes a willingness to accept your idea? Don't run down like an unwound clock. End with a spurt of ideas and enthusiasm.

4. Next go through and—

Eliminate all "verys." (Newspaper rule: "Use 'very' only once a week.")

Get rid of generalities. General words are a resource of those who seek to disarm opposition—to veil unpleasant facts. Use specific words when you wish to communicate your meaning exactly. Example: "A large steel company." More specific—"The largest steel company in the United States." Absolutely specific—"The United States Steel Corporation."

Try to eliminate all fuzzy, abstract words and expressions, and replace them with concrete words and expressions. (Test: Do the words bring up a word picture—a visual image? Example: abstract, "slavery"; concrete, "men in chains at the slave auction.")

Cut out unnecessary adjectives—which means most of them.

Be ruthless with "bromides" (hackneyed and lifeless expressions, clichés, stereotyped words and phrases). For instance, avoid "each and every," "to make a long story short," "as a matter of fact," "to begin with," "in conclusion," "leave with you," "to my mind," "without further ado," "in the last analysis," "by leaps and bounds," and "purely and simply"—to give just a few.

See if you can eliminate the first paragraph of your talk. One of the standard rules for writing a sales letter is: "Write the letter the way you think it ought to be and then cross out the first paragraph." This practically always results in a better letter. Try it on the conviction part of your sales talk.

Determine which point in your talk will be the most interesting to your prospect. Then use that in the opening paragraph of the conviction part of your sales talk.

See where you can jounce your prospect now and then. Wake him up!

D. Is the tone of your sales talk right?

1. Is the tone "I" or "you?" (Are you thinking about the prospect—or yourself?)

2. Are you super-sincere in everything you say, or are you trying to put something over on your prospect? The salesman who tells his prospect something he doesn't believe is no better than a public liar.

3. Is it positive (or negative)? Does it portray advantages to be gained or evils to be avoided? (Either may be desirable, but be sure you know what you are doing.)

4. Have you asserted anything debatable—anything to which this prospect can say, "That isn't exactly true," or "I doubt it," or "No"? (Opinions differ on this. Ben Franklin says one thing, Richard C. Borden another. My personal inclination is in favor of so modifying your statements that nobody can say, "That's untrue." (Example: If you say, "In my opinion, liquor is a curse," nobody can argue with you. Read Ben Franklin's autobiography for his reasons.)

5. Are you telling the exact truth (in accordance with the facts of the case and proved true by other statements) and will the prospect recognize it and believe it is true? Even if it is true, don't use it if it does not sound true.

6. Does it affirm confidently—has it an authoritative tone? (It will have, if you have ten times as many facts as you can use.)

7. Is there anything about it to irritate anyone?

Is it courteous? Good-natured? Frank?

Is it too clever? (Cut out any remarks you suspect of being smart or cynical.)

Have you tried to be funny? (It's a triumph if you succeed, but it's a calamity if you fail!)

Is it too familiar? (Don't be too distant—but don't verbally sit on your prospect's lap.)

E. How to make your closing effective.

1. If possible, save up a really strong appeal to use near the close.

2. Close by contrast. (See also Chapter XVI, the Close by Contrast.)

F. After it is written, ask yourself:

1. "Is it cut down to limits fixed by its live interest and importance to the prospect? Can I deliver it within the time that is likely to be at my disposal under ordinary conditions?" Remember, it is safer to cut it down while you are preparing it than while you are delivering it.

2. See if you can sum up this conviction part of your sales talk in one sentence. You may not be able to, but it is good practice.

3. Ask yourself, "Why should my prospect *remember* this sales talk?" (If you can give him nothing to remember and no reason for remembering it, why talk at all?)

4. Let it cool off a day. Then—

Give it a quick reading. How does it sound? (If it sounds terrible, don't throw it away—but go to work on it.)

Get in the probable frame of mind of your prospect and read it slowly and carefully. Ask yourself:

(*a*) "How will it sound to the prospects to whom I am to deliver it?" (You have to make certain changes in order to make your talk appropriate in various sections and to various groups of people. That is, the talk you make to a buyer of a big city department store would probably differ in some points from that which you would make to the proprietor of a small country general store.)

(*b*) "Does it contain an appeal that would convince me if I were the prospect?" (If *you* would not buy it, why should anybody?)

Get someone unfamiliar with it to read it aloud to you. Cut out or rephrase—

Anything he stumbles over.

Anything not conversational—especially "fine writing" and grandiloquent, pompous, turgid language.

Pass it around and ask others to point out the flaws.

Take a large black pencil and cut out about half of it. It is too long. Like this chapter!

Maxims

In your sales talk, strive for strength, not length.

Have you ever figured out why the sales ideas that are so sweet in your head come out so sour?

Dr. Frank Crane said: "Most salesmen lack imagination—they cannot conceive the extent of my ignorance."

Unless one is a genius, it is best to aim at being intelligible.

Talk 50 per cent less than your prospect; think 50 per cent more.

CHAPTER TWELVE

The Five Vital Rules for Convincing

But far more numerous was the herd of such
Who think too little and who talk too much.
—DRYDEN.

Here are the points to remember about the conviction part of your sales talk—the points on which most salesmen should start drilling themselves:

1. Write out the conviction part of your sales talk—and work over it until you know it almost by heart.

2. Put in plenty of examples.

3. Picture the prospect as already owning the article you are trying to sell and then tell him how it will serve him.

4. Avoid generalities—be specific.

5. Make it short.

Maxims

"Questions are never indiscreet. Answers sometimes are."
—OSCAR WILDE.

"Let a fool hold his tongue and he will pass for a sage."—
PUBLILIUS SYRUS.

"Better to remain silent and be thought a fool than to speak out and remove all doubt."—LINCOLN.

"The secret of being a bore is to tell everything."—VOL-
TAIRE.

If prospects would jump out of a five-story window to
avoid you, depend upon it, you are a bore!

The salesman who knows when to say nothing shows a fine
command of language.

"Some people can stay longer in an hour than others can
in a week."—WILLIAM DEAN HOWELLS.

Every good product needs examples more than arguments.

CHAPTER THIRTEEN

How to Arouse Desire

Persuade people to want what they already need.
—E. St. Elmo Lewis.

Great Rule 4: *To arouse desire, first determine the buying motive of your prospect. Then take these three steps:*

1. Point out the prospect's lack or want or need for the article you are selling.

2. Tell him how your article will supply that want.

3. Paint a word picture of his satisfaction or gratification as a result of buying your product.

The new salesman has finished the conviction part of his sales talk. All has gone well thus far. He has won attention, he has gained interest, he has satisfied the prospect that his goods will do all he claims for them.

"What do I do next?" he asks.

Or more probably he does not ask at all, but pulls out his order blank instead—and then wonders why he does not get the order.

Your prospect will buy your goods only if he wants them—desires them.

"If that be true," you say, "how can I make my prospects desire what I am selling?"

In a recent book on selling I found this not too helpful suggestion: "Create desire with a few well-chosen words."

Yes—but what words?

In "The Art of Persuading People," James A. Worsham gives this principle for arousing desire: "Individuals (or masses of people) are persuaded through the influence of the things they want. In actual operation this means: find out what people *want* (not merely what they *need*); be in a position to convince them that what you offer will satisfy the want, and place your proposition within their reach."

Let me tell you first that people will not desire your goods merely because they are excellent. A lot of the dullest salesmanship in the United States could be abolished if salesmen would recognize this fact. You might give me fifty reasons why the lollypop you are offering me is the best lollypop in the world, but still I don't want it. I have just eaten a large meal. I do not lack a lollypop. I don't desire it—not even with all its possible fifty points of excellence.

If You Don't Sell Your Prospect, Somebody Else May

Salesmen skip the desire step of their sales talk more often than any other.

"Yet they sell," you object.

True. People, fortunately for poor salesmen, sometimes develop their own desire.

When I bought my first car, I walked into a showroom, pointed out the one I wanted and said, "I'll take this one." The salesman did not appear in the transaction at all. I bought my first radio, my first vacuum cleaner, my first washing machine, and my first dictating machine the same way. Advertising had developed my desire.

W. J. Cameron, speaking on the Ford hour, December 4,

1938, said: "About 65 per cent of the motor cars sold today are bought by people who walk unsolicited into dealers' places of business. In all lines supposedly dependent on salesmanship, about 70 per cent of sales are not strictly sales at all, but purchases made on the initiative of the purchasers themselves."

This explains how salesmen can make sales without bothering to arouse desire. How many more sales could they make, however, if they did bother? Vastly more! Many men have more than doubled their earnings by applying the Five Great Rules—and the greatest of all these rules is the rule for arousing desire.

Should Jobbers' Salesmen Learn This Rule?

"Surely I can skip this rule," say the jobbers' salesmen. "You couldn't make a grocer or a hardware merchant desire anything I have to sell."

Maybe not—but they desire the money they could make by selling your goods.

Yes, people buy things because they *want* them—even dealers! A salesman's job is to make them *want* to buy. And this is the chapter that tells you how.

Maybe you will not use this step on every call; but if you learn it, you will certainly be able to use it often.

Follow the Formula Until It Becomes Automatic

Knowing salesmen, I know that the next question most of you will ask is this: "Do you mean to tell me that I should say to myself, 'Now then, I must arouse the desire of this man'—and then start off deliberately to take Step One?"

That is just exactly what I do mean! And I mean to have you keep on doing it consciously and painstakingly until you learn to do it automatically—until your subconscious mind has taken over the job.

Too many men trust to luck in selling—too few trust to formulas. This is also true in other fields.

George Trevor, in his golf column in the New York *Sun*, told how Walter J. Travis, probably the greatest putter ever developed in America, putted.

First he would determine the line by sighting behind the ball. Next he would study the roll of the green. Then he would examine the grass. Fourth, if a strong cross wind was blowing, he would test its velocity. Next he would mentally mark the line. Then he would place his putter in front of the ball. Next he would place the blade behind the ball. He would then determine how hard to hit the ball. Then he would fix his eye on the ball and make the stroke. This was a serious ritual, never undertaken carelessly or hurriedly.

The first putt on each green usually corresponds with the desire step in the sales talk. Both are equally important in their respective fields. Both are worth the trouble of learning a formula—then consciously sticking to that formula until you have learned to do it without conscious mental effort.

Do you remember when as a youngster you learned to tie your shoelaces? Your mother didn't say, "Be sure to tie a bow knot," and then go away and leave you to work it out for yourself.

Oh, no. She showed you the steps: "Make a single knot, hold that in place with the first finger of your right hand. Then make a loop with the left lace," and so on. You painstakingly memorized the formula. Then slowly, consciously, and timidly you went through the steps. You kept on doing it —consciously—over and over again. Finally what happened? One day you tied your laces without thinking. Tying your shoelaces had become automatic.

In learning to arouse desire, you use the same learning technique. First you memorize the formula; then you take the steps consciously again and again, until you learn to do it without conscious mental effort. When that time comes, you have probably become a salesman.

Here Is How to Take Step One

Here's the way to arouse desire:

First, determine the prospect's dominant buying motive.

"Dominant buying motive" always seemed a complicated sort of title—but is quite clear as to meaning. A buying motive is something that moves us to buy, and a dominant motive is one that has the controlling influence in moving us. Other motives besides the dominant one may play some part in influencing the decision, but the dominant motive is the one which most interests the salesman because it most affects the sale.

Dominant buying motives are no new invention. Baltasar Gracian, in "The Art of Worldly Wisdom," published in 1653, wrote:

First guess a man's ruling passion, appeal to it by word, set it in motion by temptation, and you will infallibly give checkmate to his freedom of will. Find out each man's thumbscrew. You must know where to get at any one. All men are idolaters, some of fame, others of self-interest, most of pleasure. Skill consists in knowing these idols in order to bring them into play. Knowing any man's mainspring of motive you have as it were the key to his will.

Why Are Dominant Buying Motives Important?

Why is it so important to know the prospect's dominant buying motive?

Let's take an example: A bachelor saves his first $100. The motive is probably fear—fear of hunger in his old age, fear of the poorhouse. Ten years later he has put away $50,000, let us say, but he continues to save. The motive, however, is different. He no longer fears starvation. Possibly his dominant motive now is love of ease and luxury. He wants, for his old age, not merely enough food—he wants golf, fishing, travel, other pleasures.

If you were soliciting savings accounts, and if you went to that man when he was dominated by fear of a penniless old age and talked to him about saving enough money so he could spend his winters in Florida, you would waste your talk—you would be appealing to the wrong motive. When he is worth $50,000, however, his dominant buying motive has changed. If you talked to him about putting enough money away to keep him out of the poorhouse—you would waste your breath.

So be sure you know the prospect's dominant buying motive before you try to close the deal.

Consider This World-famous Selling Job

Take for example one of the most famous selling jobs in history—the job of selling Ferdinand and Isabella the idea of financing Columbus's trip to find a new route to India.

Columbus worked six years at this selling job. At the

end of that time he was convinced that the Spanish mon-
archs would not buy it, and so he determined to go to France
and see if his selling technique would be more successful
there.

What follows (except for certain matter in parentheses, in
which I point out the buying motives which were appealed to
in this historic sales talk) is from "The Life and Voyages of
Christopher Columbus," by Washington Irving.

The "Closer" in This Sale Was Luis de St. Angel

When the new friends who were zealous believers in the theory
of Columbus saw him really on the point of abandoning the country,
they were filled with distress. . . . Among the number was Luis de
St. Angel, receiver of the ecclesiastical revenues in Aragon. Determined if possible to avert the evil, he obtained an immediate audience of the queen, accompanied by Alonzo de Quintanilla. The
exigency of the moment gave him courage and eloquence.

Note How He Used Buying Motives

He did not confine himself to entreaties but almost mingled re-
proaches, expressing astonishment that a queen who had evinced
the spirit to undertake so many great and perilous enterprises,
should hesitate at one where the loss could be so trifling, while the
gain might be incalculable [motive—desire for gain]. He reminded
her how much might be done for the glory of God, the exaltation
of the Church [motive—advancement of religion], and the exten-
sion of her own power and dominion [motive—desire to be more
important]. What cause of regret to herself, of triumph to her
enemies, of sorrow to her friends, should this enterprise, thus re-
jected by her, be accomplished by some other power! [Motive—
rivalry and fear of loss.] He reminded her what fame and dominion

other princes had acquired by their discoveries; here was an opportunity to surpass them all [appeal to competitive spirit]. It was worth the trouble and expense to clear up even a doubt upon a matter of such importance, for it belonged to enlightened and magnanimous princes to investigate questions of the kind, and to explore the wonders and secrets of the universe [appeal to pride].

These and many more arguments were urged with that persuasive power which honest zeal imparts. The generous spirit of Isabella was enkindled. It seemed as if, for the first time, the subject broke on her mind in its real grandeur, and she declared her resolution to undertake the enterprise.

Isabella Signs on the Dotted Line

There was still a moment's hesitation. The king looked coldly on the affair, and the royal finances were absolutely drained by the war. Some time must be given to replenish them. How could she draw on the exhausted treasury for a measure to which the king was adverse. St. Angel watched this suspense with trembling anxiety. The next moment reassured him. With an enthusiasm worthy of herself, and of the cause, Isabella exclaimed, "I undertake the enterprise for my own crown of Castile, and will pledge my jewels to raise the necessary funds." This was the proudest moment in the life of Isabella; it stamped her renown forever as the patroness of the discovery of the New World.

How to Learn the Prospect's Dominant Buying Motive

From these examples it is easy to understand why it is necessary to learn the dominant buying motive of your prospect before you try to arouse his desire.

How do you find it out? Well, sometimes you don't—generally you do.

If you are selling something that costs a considerable

amount of money, you will take pains to find out your prospect's dominant buying motive before you try to sell. If you are selling an article of smaller price, you will perhaps have to learn his motive as you go along.

For example, you are trying to sell a man a residence. You would want to know whether the prospect's dominant buying motive is, say love of family or the desire to feel important. Surely you could easily determine this by asking a few questions. This prospect would, if you asked him, tell you what points he wanted in a house—and in doing so he would almost certainly reveal his dominant buying motive.

All right, you now have the information you need to start arousing desire, and you take the first of the three steps.

Why Must You Point Out the Want?

STEP ONE: *Point out to the prospect his lack of, or want for, the article or service you are selling.*

Does this step make sense?

Hobbes, writing over 300 years ago, said, "Desire is the craving for something not possessed."

Look back to some purchase of yours that ran into money —a radio, air conditioning, an oil burner, an electric refrigerator, an automobile, or a home—and ask yourself if the first step in your desire for that article was not a realization of a want or lack. Didn't you say to yourself, "Other people have this—I lack it"?

All desire is built on a feeling of lack or want or longing.

The salesman's job may be to point out the lack—or it may be to intensify the feeling of lack.

A writer in *Manager's Magazine* said:

"One of the best salesmen I know has this motto hanging over his desk: 'The best way to make a sale is first to find out what problem a man is worrying about, and then to show him how what you have to sell will solve his problem.' "

He is dead right.

We can go a step further and say that frequently it helps to call to a man's attention something about which he should be worrying but isn't.

Politicians recognize this point. Take, as an example, the Townsend Plan. Old people didn't know they had a desire to have the government support them in luxury—until their attention was called to it by Dr. Townsend and his fellow sleight-of-hand artists. Or take the idea of spending your way out of a depression—no desire existed for that technique until it was sold to the country by the press agents of the New Deal.

If They're Cold, Turn on the Heat

George H. Harris, a successful life underwriter, is quoted by Maxwell Droke as follows:

I never hesitate to employ emotional appeal. When the situation demands it, I bear down with a good deal of force. Sometimes the picture I am obliged to paint is not a pleasant one.

"Go 'way," one prospect said to me. "You make me miserable."

"Good," I replied. "When you are so miserable you can't sleep at night, call me up and I'll write your policy."

What was Harris doing? He was taking the first step of arousing desire—he was pointing out to the prospect his lack of life insurance.

As E. St. Elmo Lewis says, "Salesmanship is the ability to

persuade people to want what they need." (And, apparently, sometimes what they don't need.)

For example, a third of a century ago practically nobody desired radios. Nobody felt the lack of them. Popular-priced radios didn't exist, so nobody called your attention to your lack of a radio and you didn't feel any lack.

Finally, however, radios became practical. We found that our neighbors owned them, so we began to feel our lack—and finally we bought. Or maybe it was a salesman who did the job of pointing out the lack.

Let's take another example of pointing out a want.

Suppose you are selling oil burners. You might say, "With your present equipment you have to get up at five o'clock in the morning and open up the furnace and put on coal, in order to have the house warm when the children get up. Your wife sometimes has to shovel on coal in the afternoon. When you are away on trips, either your wife has to take over the whole job of tending to the furnace— shoveling on coal, shoveling out ashes—or you have to hire somebody to do it. The temperature of your house, of course, is uneven. You are too hot in the forenoon, too cold in the afternoon. Getting out ashes is a dirty job—one that you don't enjoy."

In other words, you were pointing out what is wrong with his present situation. You were trying to dissatisfy him with his present heating equipment. You were pointing out his lack. You were taking the first step toward arousing desire.

How Can Your Prospect Supply That Lack?

STEP TWO: *Tell your prospect how your goods or service will supply his lack.*

The next, or second, step is quite natural if you will only ask yourself, "What is my prospect thinking?"

If you have carried him along through the first step he is now thinking, "Yes, that's right. Conditions with respect to this matter are not too satisfactory. I don't like to get up at five o'clock to start a furnace," or "I don't like to drive a disreputable-looking old car," or "I don't like my accounting department always to be behind."

If you have made your prospect feel his lack, then your next step is the entirely obvious one of pointing out that your goods or service will supply this lack.

You say, for example: "Install the XYZ Oil Burner and your heating troubles are over. Once you have put in a supply of oil and wound your thermostat clock you can forget it. At five o'clock in the morning the heat comes on. It stays on until the house is warm enough. Then it automatically shuts off. If the house falls below the temperature you want, the furnace comes on again. . . ."

You have taken the second step—you have shown how your article or service will supply the lack. This is a simple, easy, obvious step.

Can You Paint a Word Picture?

NOW FOR THE THIRD STEP: *Paint a word picture of the satisfaction or gratification of your prospect as a result of buying your goods or service.*

Let's start with an example of the third step of *arousing* desire as it could be taken by an oil-burner salesman. Here it is:

Suppose you have just installed your new oil burner. At five o'clock in the morning, if you were in your cellar, you would hear a little click, the motor would turn over, an electric flash would start the oil burning. After that, all you would hear—even in the cellar—would be the comforting noise of a good oil fire. But you wouldn't be in your cellar—you would be in your bed. There you would hear nothing until steam began to come out of the radiator valve. Then you would pop out of bed, pull down the windows, duck back into bed and tuck the covers up around your chin and go back to sleep. When your alarm clock went off and you threw back the covers, you would step out into a warm room. Your clothes would be warm. You would dress in a room at a temperature of seventy. You would go to the thermometer and look—to be sure. Then you would look at the outdoor thermometer. Suppose it was ten above. You couldn't even shiver at the thought—you would be too comfortable.

This is probably not all the salesman would say in this step of his sales talk, but it is enough to illustrate the point.

What did the salesman do? He painted a word picture of the prospect getting up on a cold morning in a warm room. It was a picture of his satisfaction as a result of having installed an oil burner.

This Step Calls for a Little Imagination

"Why do I paint this word picture of the prospect's satisfaction?" you ask.

Because the best way to arouse desire is to pick up the prospect mentally and carry him into the future and let him see himself enjoying what you are trying to sell him. It is an appeal to the heart. Sir John Lubbock said: "You are more likely to carry men with you by enlisting their feelings than by convincing their reason." Surely this is true in the semifinal step of your sales talk.

Think of your own case. Before you bought your first automobile, didn't you have mind pictures of yourself driving the car around—on business or pleasure? Before you bought your first radio, didn't you have a picture of yourself sitting in front of a fire, listening? Couldn't you, in your mind, hear the wonderful programs coming right into your own living room?

Perhaps the prospect at this point will paint his own mind pictures—but the wise salesman does not take a chance. He does the painting himself.

Don't Sell the Car, Sell the Scenery

In "Successful Salesmen's Experiences," Bob Allen, Ray-bestos-Manhattan, Inc., Seattle, wrote:

I am a great believer of indirect selling. By this I mean painting a mental picture in the prospect's mind of the joy, the comfort, the profit, the security, or whatever the appeal the product I am selling should have for the prospective buyer.

Some years ago I was selling automobiles in a small country town. As I did not have a prospect on file to call on, I drove out into the country. I saw a good-size ranch, drove in, and introduced myself to the farmer. He laughed when I told him whom I represented and said that he had a better automobile than the one I was selling. Naturally, I was interested in seeing something better than mine and found that he had a higher priced car about ten years old. It was very well kept and looked like a new car with very little mileage on it.

I knew it would be impossible to trade with him but could not understand why he did not use it more. I found that he had a wife and two children and had hardly taken them out of town. I told him that it was not fair to his wife and family not to visit the many beauty spots of the West, which I described in detail, while he could still go with them. I did not attempt to sell him, but on leaving I gave him one of my catalogues.

The next morning, he came into my salesroom and said, "We have decided to take a trip and see all those beautiful places you spoke about and Mama wants this green one with the trunk on back."

Here's an example as told by O. T. Carter, then a salesman for a trucking company, at a meeting of a Dale Carnegie Selling School Class in Cleveland in 1939:

The next day after we were given the rule for arousing desire in this class, the boss called me in his office and said, "O. T., do you want to go out on a forlorn hope?" I answered, "No, I don't want to, but I will."

"Here's the problem," he went on. "A man and his family living here in Cleveland are moving to Los Angeles. The expenses are being paid by the company for which this man works. They have already closed a deal with another company—at a price lower than we can quote. Go out and see if you can do anything to get the job for us."

I went out, talked with the woman of the family, and persuaded her to switch the job to us and to pay the difference out of her own pocket.

I was so astonished at my success that after the order was signed, I asked this woman what had decided her to make the change.

She answered, "When you told me how your truck would back up in front of my new home in Los Angeles, and how your men would carry those containers with my dresses in them up into my room, and when you pictured how nice and fresh my dresses would look when they came out of their special containers—well, that was when I decided to have your trucks carry my stuff."

Only a word picture! But it closed a difficult sale.

Appeal to the Senses

How do you paint word pictures?

Let's ask ourselves again what we want our prospect to

think? We want him to see himself using this article or service—we want him to see it in his mind's eye, to hear it in his mind's ear, to taste it in his mind's mouth, or to smell it in his mind's nose.

Let's take first the matter of arousing visual images—of bringing a picture to the mind's eye of your prospect. Let's go back to the oil-burner example: You might say, "By seven o'clock in the morning the temperature of your house will be 70." That is a specific statement—but it is not concrete—it does not bring up a word picture. Suppose, instead, you say, "When you walk downstairs into your living room you take down the thermometer and walk over to the light and look at it carefully. You find the column of mercury is not merely near the 70 mark—the top of it is exactly at the 70 mark." Note the difference. In the second example you have given your prospect a word picture of himself looking at the thermometer.

Or suppose in the same sales talk you want to bring a picture to the mind's ear. You might say, "You're still in bed, but what's the cheerful sound you hear? A comforting sizzle of steam in your radiator valve, maybe a little pounding in the pipes—just enough to wake you up so you can close your window and shut out the cold morning wind that is howling and whistling around the eaves of your house." Maybe that's a little flowery, but it illustrates the point. You made him hear the valve sizzle and the wind whistle.

Do you want to appeal to the sense of feeling? All right, why not say, "Try putting your hand on the radiator—only be ready to get it off fast, because by now it is probably blistering hot."

Don't Skip This Step

Salesmen rebel against taking this third step. Why? I don't know, but I suspect because it calls for a little imagination and a little effort.

The salesmen who have used it find that it produces results which are little short of marvelous.

H. G. Wells wanted to carry his readers far into the future. So he invented the time machine. The hero gets in the machine, throws a lever, and soon is in the year 802,701 A.D. Wells then gives his readers a word picture of the people of that day.

The salesman's job is to get into his time machine and to journey into the future and then to come back and give his prospect a word picture of what he saw. Be sure the prospect is the hero of the picture.

Try it, I beg of you. Use it just a few times, by way of satisfying yourself that it works. Watch your prospect when you begin to project him into the future—when you bring up before his eyes a picture of himself doing what he wants to do, note his intense interest.

The Emotional Appeal Gets 'Em!

As D. B. Taylor pointed out in a *Printers' Ink* article, sales are not made by a high-pressure close but by painting an alluring word picture. Says Mr. Taylor:

Look at the methods of the highest pressure artists of all—the confidence men. . . . They always select such "products" as have great emotional appeal. . . . Always the confidence man paints a word picture of what possession will do. . . . He paints the word picture and the prospect sells himself.

When he sells the Brooklyn Bridge, what does he talk about? He gives his prospect a visualization of the delightful position of being able to exact a toll from all who cross.

He paints the word picture and the prospect sells himself.

Start Using This Rule—It Works

Stop right now and do some thinking about this. Determine to try it tomorrow, if only on one prospect. Think right now of some prospect you are going to try to close tomorrow. What does he lack that your goods or service will supply? How will your goods or service supply that lack? All right, now stop and paint that word picture.

Remember, it is not a word picture unless your prospect can see it in his mind's eye, and it is not a truly effective word picture unless he can actually *see himself* in the picture.

Suppose, to take a new example, you are selling dictating machines. In this case you might say: "This machine will save your secretary an hour a day." That is specific but not concrete. It brings an idea to mind—but not a word picture. If you wanted to bring a word picture, you might say, "The mail is put on your desk in the morning and you call your secretary. She pulls up a chair, sits down, opens her book, and sits poised to take your first letter. But the phone rings. You turn, pick up the receiver and talk for ten minutes with a prospect. Meanwhile your secretary sits in her chair, juggling her pencils, patting her hair, looking back over some dead notes, and examining her fingernails. And, at the end of the week, you hand her a check for $50—for doing just that."

That is a word picture—maybe not a good one, but at least one that brings a picture to your mind's eye.

If you will (*a*) make your prospect recognize his lack of your goods, if (*b*) you show that your goods will supply this lack, if (*c*) you will then paint a word picture of his satisfaction or gratification—then, if ever, you will have aroused desire. Then your prospect really wants your goods, really longs for them.

What Do Purchasing Agents "Long For"?

"Pshaw," you say, "I sell to purchasing agents—they don't long for anything but low prices."

Joking aside, who writes the requisition? Suppose you are selling a typewriter. To you, the typewriters you are selling may be just a piece of machinery on which you make a commission. To the purchasing agent they may be just another item on which he can shave the price down a few dollars and thus earn credit with the treasurer. But to the girls who sit in front of them all day (and to the head of the typing department), a good typewriter plays a big part in their satisfaction and efficiency. You can hold them breathless with a word picture of a typist writing on an efficient, easy-writing machine. The same is true of the head of the typing department. She may not use the machine herself—but paint a word picture of work coming through faster, a word picture of cleaner, neater letters, a picture of typists fresh at the day's end— paint a picture like that and you arouse her desire to equip her department with your machines.

If you sell only to purchasing agents, if you cannot possibly get to users, to those who write the requisitions, or to the people who do the planning and the execution, then you don't need to know much about selling anyway—but you ought to know a lot about human relations.

How Jobbers' Salesmen Can Use This Step

Naturally, the jobbers' salesman rarely uses this step with the elaborate detail of, say, an insurance salesman. But he can often use it—if he will.

The jobbers' salesman has to *sell*—reluctant as he often is to admit it. When he has to make a real sale, then he needs all five steps, and this one most of all.

Suppose a jobbers' salesman is trying to get a grocer to stock a high-priced article, he might say, at the desire step:

You say that you are not getting the high-class trade of your neighborhood?

If you stocked goods that appealed to a higher class trade, you would certainly begin to get more of it.

Suppose we circularize the high-grade buyers in this territory and let them know that you carry this line. Mrs. Jones up here on Wildwood Plaza opens her mail some morning and reads that your store now stocks our line. Some of our magazine advertisements flash into her mind. So when she goes out to do her buying, she heads for your store. She walks in, asks for this line—but she doesn't stop there. She strolls around your store to see what else you carry. . . .

You have painted a word picture of his satisfaction as a result of buying what you are offering.

Of course it works for jobbers' salesmen—if they will let it.

It Works Miracles for All Salesmen

All right, you now have an unfailing rule for arousing desire. Will you use it? Will you at least *try* it? Will you take all three steps—not just the first two? Will you persist in it until it becomes second nature to use it? If you will, I can almost guarantee that you will increase sales and earnings.

Maxims

You can make anybody want to buy anything by putting the right idea into his head.

Your customer wants to buy. He'll deny it—but you keep on thinking it anyway.

"Let your imagination carry you into the clouds—but keep your feet on the ground."—CHARLES L. GOULD.

CHAPTER FOURTEEN

More Rules for Making the Prospect Want to Buy

Nothing troubles you for which you do not yearn.
—CICERO.

Now for a few of the minor rules for arousing desire:

In the desire step, make your appeal to a man's emotions, not his brain—to his heart, not his head. You want to make him *feel*, not *think*. Don't reason with him—don't argue with him. Point out his lack, paint a word picture of his satisfaction, project him into the future and paint a word picture of him enjoying himself—and then look for miracles.

Manager's Magazine said, "Ninety per cent of all life insurance sold results from an appeal to the heart, rather than the head."

Talk more about *wants* than *needs*. When I started selling securities with a small sales force, the worst competitor we had was not some other security—but automobiles. Our prospects lacked a good security, they *needed* a retirement fund, but they *wanted* an automobile. So most of them bought the automobile.

Try to make your prospect feel that he is losing something —doing without something he really ought to have—when he does not buy your goods. Make it vivid. Make it concrete. Make him see himself losing it. Maybe he is losing the pro-

121

tection of financial statements because they do not come out on time. Maybe he is sending out smudgy form letters because his equipment is obsolete. Maybe his business is losing the profits that would come if he stocked your nationally advertised line. In other words, make him feel dissatisfied.

Lots of us were satisfied with cars that started with a crank (if they did start!) until a salesman came along and sold us a feeling of dissatisfaction—and new cars with self-starters.

Here's a good rule from Charles W. Mears: "All the while you are speaking, act as though all that you suggested were the most plausible, reasonable things possible. You are his friend, serving his best interests." Unless you are the prospect's friend, unless you are honestly trying to serve his best interests you deserve to fail.

Never try to be logical in the desire step of your sales talk. You are appealing to the heart. Desire is not logical. The heart is not logical. To paraphrase Spinoza, we don't *want* a thing because it is good, but we feel it is good *because we want it*.

You Can't Do It with Arguments

A diner said to the waitress, "I object to an omelet filled with jelly."

"You don't like jelly?" inquired the waitress.

"Yes, I like it very much."

"Then you don't like omelet?"

"Yes, I like omelet too."

"Then you must like jelly omelet."

"Well, I don't."

The waitress just couldn't make the patron like jelly omelet by logic. She couldn't *argue* him into desire.

Remember, you are not trying to make your prospect *recognize* the existence of a lack with his brain, but to *feel* the lack with his heart. You could say, "It is extremely uncomfortable to get up in a cold room." That would be an appeal to the brain—and how colorless it is! If you say, "The alarm clock goes off and you throw back the cover and stand up on the cold floor. B-r-r-r-r! You dash to the windows. The cold hits you in the chest and almost knocks your wind out"—that is appealing to the sensations of sight and feeling.

Be enthusiastic. A successful salesman once said: "In checking back over my sales, I find that my best days were those when I was never conscious of trying to sell anything, but when I was tremendously enthused over an opportunity to help my customers make money."

You should be conscious that you are trying to arouse the prospect's desire—but *he* shouldn't. You are quite safe if you are thinking in terms of your prospect's interests.

If you are thinking at this point, "If I can make this man really want this item, I'll get the order and commission," then you are likely to be too eager and to warn the prospect not to buy. If, instead, you are thinking, "This article will really do for this man just what he wants done, this future I am painting him is true, I am honestly trying to help him"— then you need not worry about being too eager.

Maxims

If you manage yourself, the interview will manage itself.

Aim facts at the mind, fears at the heart.

"You cannot demonstrate or prove an aspiration."—JOHN MORLEY.

You can't *make* them buy it; but you can make them *want* it.

People don't buy because they know all the facts. They buy because they *want* what you sell.

CHAPTER FIFTEEN

The Secrets of Closing

A good sales talk is a good thing, but the signed order is the *thing.*

Great Rule 5: *Get a decision in your favor by weighing the ideas in favor of buying against those opposed to buying.*

Suppose you have decided to go to Africa to take photographs of tigers in their native jungles. You buy your equipment, pack, sail to Africa, transport yourself and your party and luggage to the edge of the jungle, find a good location, and set up your camera. When the camera is ready, you climb into a seat you have built in a tree and settle down for a long wait.

Finally you hear the tiger coming. Naturally your heart beats faster. In a few seconds now you will have your pictures —or a failure.

You are not unnecessarily alarmed. You have planned it all carefully. Your equipment is right, your camera is properly set, and there comes the tiger.

Isn't this comparable to a sale—except that in the case cited above, all the tiger gets out of it is a scare—and the publicity?

In the case of the sales talk you have taken all the necessary preliminary steps. You know your product. You know your prospect. You have given him reasons for buying. You have aroused desire. Now you are going to ask for the order.

Of course your heart beats a little faster. In a few minutes you will know whether you made the sale—or whether you didn't.

The closing, however, is not some great, amazing, astounding, separate act. It is merely one step in a process.

A resident of San Francisco took a country cousin to see the San Francisco-Oakland Bridge.

"That," said the Californian, "is the longest bridge in the world."

"Shucks," answered the country cousin, "it's nothing but a lot of little bridges strung together."

And a complete sales talk is just a lot of little sales talks strung together, and the last "bridge" is closing.

If you have taken the other steps properly, you have a right to expect success—not every time, but often enough so that you can sell profitably.

Take an analogous case: In making certain kinds of cakes, the baking powder is the last ingredient to go in. It is the closing step. If you forget it, your cake is dough. On the other hand, it is no separate miracle. If you have taken the other steps properly, then add the baking powder if you expect a good cake. If you have left out some other important ingredient, then no amount of baking powder will save the cake.

The beginner usually looks upon closing as some sort of a private miracle that experienced salesmen know how to perform. The beginners want to know how they too can perform this miracle.

Closing Is Just One Step in a Process

Closing is not magic. You cannot, by any trickery known to man, get any material number of orders from people who are not willing to buy.

If you have built up the willingness in the previous step, then closing is easy. If you haven't, then it matters little how you close, because you are not going to get the order anyway.

Did you ever try to drive a pig (or preferably a disagreeable old boar) into a pen? If not, you have missed one of life's great experiences. The pig may go peaceably along the road for half a mile or so—just to make you feel as though he had bought the idea of going where you want him to go. Then you come to the pen—and the pig refuses! If the refusal is firm and if the pig is large, it will probably take ten men and a vast amount of perspiration to get the pig inside.

In this case, the preliminary steps have not been properly taken. You haven't built up the pig's desire to go in. If you had kept him on short rations for a couple of days, then laid a train of shelled corn into the pen—if you had properly taken the previous steps of the selling process—you would not have had to make the "sale" by force.

Take the matter of getting married—one of the big sales climaxes of most men's lives. The deal is actually closed when the girl says, "I do." But you, the groom, are not nervous when that moment arrives (or anyhow, not nervous as to whether or not she will say, "I do"!) You have carried her along through the steps of the courtship, from that first good-night kiss right up to now. Her dotted-line remark, "I do," is just an incident in a long selling campaign. It would be a calamity not to get it—but it's nothing to worry about. If the rest of your campaign has been well handled, if your prospect has gone along with you through the other steps of the matrimonial sale, she is not likely to refuse at "I do." For one girl who refuses at that point, there are ten million who don't!

This rule applies to all salesmen—specialty, jobbers', door-to-door—every time they get up to the point of asking for the order. (It does not apply to the jobbers' salesman when he is merely taking orders—it does apply to him when he actually sells.)

"I'm Ready to Close—What Do I Say?"

Let's assume you feel that you have a chance of success and ask, "What must I say to get the order? How is it done?"

I went around for years asking people, "How do you close?" I wrote a book on selling before I was any too sure. Up to that time I had nothing but the old, reliable rule, "Ask for the order." (There are worse rules than that, too!)

Every day salesmen lose orders that are ripe to drop in their laps because they do not ask the prospect to buy. So, if you can't remember the right way to close, just ask for the order anyway.

F. McKee Smith, manager of the Jefferson Standard Life Insurance Company, Washington, D. C., tells this story:

I was selling Jordan automobiles years ago. One of our salesmen was a great orator, could talk your ear off, but couldn't sell. One day I found out why. A man came in, in mid-December, and talked about buying a Jordan for a Christmas present for his wife. My orator friend made the sale and then, to my horror, instead of asking for a deposit, said, "I'll drop in in a couple of days to talk with you about it."

So I walked up and said, "I couldn't help overhearing the conversation. We have only one of those models in that color. We couldn't possibly get another one before Christmas. If you will give me your check for $1,000, I'll have this car put in the warehouse for you."

The prospect sat down and wrote out the check.

After he was gone my friend said, "What's wrong with me?"

So I told him. "You make the sale, you don't ask for the order."

It is wise to ask for the order, but it is wiser to ask for it in the most effective way.

In my early days as a sales manager, I could not find any procedure for closing that even made sense. Finally, one day, I chanced on Norvall Hawkins's book, "The Selling Process." In it I found a rule for closing. It seemed a reasonable rule—it squared with common sense. The next day I took it out and tried it on my prospects. It did not close them all, but it closed more than any other plan I had ever heard of. I have used it ever since. Thousands of men under my direction have used it. It makes sense. It works.

It's Old But Good

The principle involved is not new. Ben Franklin wrote:

Such cases of indecision are difficult chiefly because while we have them under consideration all the reasons pro and con are not present to the mind at the same time. . . . To get over this, my way is to divide half a sheet of paper by a line into two columns; writing over the one "Pro" and over the other "Con." Then, I put down the different motives for and against the measure. When I have thus got them all together in one view I endeavor to estimate their respective

weights. I find where the balance lies . . . and come to a determination accordingly. . . ."

—From "Benjamin Franklin"—Carl Van Doren.

In the next chapter, I give you the substance of Hawkins's
rule for closing. I recommend also that you buy "The Selling
Process." You should be able to get it through any bookstore.
Before we get to the rule, however, let's have a look at some
of the problems of closing.

"The Psychological Moment" Is Not a "Moment"

Let's dispose first of that old dragon, "the psychological
moment." In my opinion, it certainly isn't a "moment" and
it probably isn't "psychological."

The person who christened it a "moment" was no judge of
time. A "moment" says Webster, is a "minute portion of
time, an instant."

Beginners hear about the psychological *moment* and feel
that they have to hit it exactly on the second—or miss it
altogether.

Are beginners right in trying to catch one single, elusive
second?

Look back to some time when you were considering some
important purchase. Somewhere along the way you perhaps
said to yourself, "He's right about this and I'm going to buy
it—even if I do have to knock my budget sideways."

Look back and ask yourself, "Was it a 'moment'?"

Is it not true that for many minutes, maybe hours, you
were ready to buy? Was it not equally true that finally, if
the order was not closed, you began to think of a lot of good
reasons why you shouldn't buy—and perhaps the "moment"

passed? Certainly, even if it passed, it was subject to revival any time the salesman gave you enough good reasons and aroused enough desire to overcome your objections.

I have seen salesmen spend so much thought in trying to guess when the psychological moment had arrived that they could not keep their minds on their sales talks.

Remember, you are not letting your prospect drift along while you talk about your product. Instead, you are *carrying* him along from step to step, always leading up to the time when you ask for the order. The efficient salesman does not wait for the psychological moment—he makes his own. So don't worry about some small fragment of time in which the order can be closed. When you finish the desire step and when all objections have been answered, unless you have good reason for believing that the prospect is not ready to close, by all means go ahead with the closing step.

Don't Talk Yourself Out of the Sale

Suppose the prospect gets ahead of you and is ready to close before you realize it—How can you avoid the danger of talking past the buying period—of missing the so-called "psychological moment"? By watching for "buying signals" and by using "trial closes."

What are the buying signals—what should the salesman watch for?

(*a*) He should watch for what the prospect *does*.

(*b*) He should note how the prospect *looks*.

(*c*) He should note what the prospect *says*.

"What is the prospect likely to do that will serve as a warning?" you ask.

If the prospect does something that indicates growing inter-est, it is a good sign. Better still, if he does something that indicates that already in his mind he owns whatever you are trying to sell him, then the time has come to close. The pros-pect may ask to drive the car around the block again, he may dictate a real letter on the dictating machine, he may examine the product more carefully.

Next watch the prospect for changes in expression. These may warn you that the time has arrived to ask for the order.

Listen Intently for "Buying Questions"

The best signal of all is often given by something the prospect says, particularly by some question he asks. If what he says indicates that mentally he has already bought your product, then waste no more time—the order probably is yours.

What is he likely to say? He may ask: "Does it get out of order easily?" "Do you supply oil with it?" "Do you install it?" "Do you have a repair department?" "Can I turn in my old machine?"

If you are selling to both a husband and wife at the same time and one says to the other, "Well, dear, what do you think?" you can be sure that one of them is sold.

Sometimes the prospect will not show by act, look, or word when he is ready to buy.

I remember almost the first preferred stock I ever sold was to a lady who lived on a farm near Augusta, Maine. It was back in the days when few farmers—and fewer salesmen—drove automobiles. When I found the lady, she was dusting off the family buggy, preparatory to driving to Augusta.

She was using one of those old-time feather dusters, with a cane handle and feathers dyed with gay colors.

She was embarrassed and so was I. I launched into my sales talk—and she went on dusting. On and on she went around the buggy, and I after her. At the end of the fourth lap I ran completely out of words, long before she ran out of dust—and I hadn't learned to ask for the order. So the conversation just ceased.

She waited politely for me to go on, but I was stuck. Then she said in a matter-of-fact way, "I'll take five shares."

If she gave any buying signal, I didn't see it. The chances are that she was ready to buy when I arrived. Perhaps if I had asked for the order at the end of the second or third lap, I'd have sold her twenty shares.

Don't Be Afraid to Ask for the Order—Often!

Have you ever seen a paragraph like this in a newspaper?

Thomas F. Jones, salesman, was shot and critically wounded by a prospect whom he had just asked for an order.

You never will.

So ask for the order.

If you do get any buying signals, you need not worry, provided you have used "trial closes."

What are trial closes? They are questions asked by the salesman at various times in his sales talk to determine whether or not his prospect is ready to buy. In general, a trial close is some question on a minor point or an alternative decision (discussed later in this chapter) such as: "Do you have your securities delivered at the house or the office?"

"Can you go over to the doctor's for an examination this morning?" "How many transcribing machines would you need?" "Would you wash your clothes this afternoon if we could deliver the washer then, or would Monday be better?"

Trial Closes Help You to Know When to Close

Why are trial closes necessary?

Well, take this example: Suppose a man calls your office and makes some vague kind of an inquiry about the article you are selling. You follow up the inquiry with a call. It may prove that your prospect is ready to buy. In that case, if you push off into a long sales talk you may talk right past the closing point and talk yourself out of the order. On the other hand, it may develop that the prospect is only mildly interested. In that case you want to shoot the whole selling process at him.

How can you be right, in either case? How can you know whether or not he is ready to sign the order blank?

By using trial closes.

After you have talked a couple of minutes you ask, "Do you like the larger size or the smaller?" If he expresses a preference, you ask, "Do you like the natural wood finish or the green?" If he again tells you what he likes, you can rightfully expect that he is ready to close, so you try another. "I think we could deliver this equipment from our warehouse this afternoon—or would Monday be soon enough?"

If the answer is, "I'd like it this afternoon," then you fill out the order blank. If he says, "Oh, I'm not going to buy any," then you are no worse off than you were before you used the trial close, and you start right back in your sales talk, just as though he had not answered you at all.

"How Soon Will You Need It?"

A paint salesman, quoted by J. C. Aspley, used to fire this question at his prospect, virtually without warning: "How soon will you need the paint?"

If the answer was, "Maybe in a couple of weeks," the salesman went ahead with the writing out of the order. If the answer was vague or even negative, the salesman went right on with his sales talk as though nothing had happened.

To sum it up: The trial close leaves you no worse off if you get a turndown; and you are vastly better off if it gets you an acceptance.

One of the cardinal sins of beginners is a failure to ask for the order. Because they are afraid, they talk on and on. Usually they get further and further away from the order the longer and longer they talk.

Ask for the order. What harm can it do? If the prospect turns you down, you're not out.

You would think, from watching some salesmen, that a No was like an electrocution—once the switch is pulled you're dead. Fortunately, a No is no more serious than a fleabite.

Get Used to Hearing "No"

If salesmen could only get clearly in mind that No is not final and irrevocable—that most sales are made after the prospect has said No at least once, often many times—they would sell more goods and waste less time.

Suppose an insurance peddler came to you and said, "You don't want to buy any insurance today, do you?" Your answer would be, "No, I don't want to buy any insurance today." Suppose he kept right on telling about your insurance lacks and needs. And suppose, after each point, he asked you for the order. What would happen, assuming he was a good salesman and that you really needed insurance? Your Noes would continue for quite a while, but each one would probably be weaker, wouldn't it?

If he stopped at the first No, or maybe the fifth, he would not make the sale. If he ignored the Noes he would probably get the order.

"Yes," you say, "but isn't it a mistake to get the prospect in the habit of saying No?"

Of course in actual selling you would so phrase your trial closings that he would find it hard to answer No.

Get over this No phobia. Get so you expect a flock of Noes before you get your Yes. Don't let them disturb you any more than a question or an objection or a mosquito bite.

Christopher Columbus got No for eighteen years before he got his Yes. "I can't wait eighteen years," you say. True —and equally you are not likely to discover another America. Admire and emulate his courage and persistency, and regret only that he was not a better salesman!

If He Wants a Cadillac Don't Offer Him a Chevrolet

One of the most useful of the trial closes is based on the size of the order, "Can you handle twenty bonds today, Mr. Blank, or will ten be enough?" "Shall we make this policy for $50,000 or for $25,000?"

One suggestion: Always ask for at least twice as much as you expect. In the securities business, back in the old days, we used to have trouble getting the salesmen to ask for large enough orders. Because the salesman himself could not buy in $10,000 lots, he could not think in $10,000 lots. When I started selling securities I always asked people to buy one share. My investment unit was $100, and so I supposed everybody's was.

People are not usually scared off by being asked to buy more of any item than they can swing. Instead they are complimented.

A great advantage of starting high is that if you get a turn-down, you can assume that the objection to buying is the objection to buying so much—and you can drop down and thereby often save the sale. A man who turns you down cold on twenty bonds may finally buy five.

Conversely, people are sometimes insulted by being asked to buy too little.

For instance, back in the thirties a friend went into the Packard showrooms in Newark and asked to see a Packard. My friend was anything but a careful dresser—but in those days he didn't have to dress well, because he was in the big money. The salesman took one look at my friend's scrubby clothes and said with a superior air, "I suppose you want a six." My friend left within five minutes—and bought a Lincoln, without bothering to ask the price!

Naturally this "start high" rule must be used with judgment. If you know a man is in the secondhand-Ford class, don't show him a Rolls-Royce!

Don't Wait—Close!

"Should I use a trial close before I make my demonstration?" you ask (assuming you are selling an article that should normally be demonstrated).

Of course, provided you have any reason for thinking that the prospect is ready to buy.

Get into the habit of slipping in trial closings all along the way.

"I could get one of these to your office by three o'clock this afternoon," said with the rising inflection of a question, may win you a favorable response. If it does, start right in closing. Don't talk past the closing point.

At a sales meeting in Bath, Maine, back in 1918, I offered a prize to the salesman of Central Maine Power Company who would bring in the first order for the company's Preferred. The salesmen went out with a rush. One of them, Perley Clark, a chronic prize winner, walked down the street to a clothing store and said to the proprietor, "Do you want to buy some stock?" "Well," said the prospect, "I was sort of figuring on buying a little." Perley whipped out his order blank, got the signature and a check, and was back in the hotel within ten minutes to collect his prize. If he had made a sales talk at that point he might have talked himself out of the sale. As it was, he got the order by starting with a trial close. He got the order, the commission, and a prize.

So much for trial closes. Let us assume that in any given sales talk you have used them and that they have not produced the desired response, that you have now answered all the prospect's objections and that you have taken the three "desire" steps. How should you ask for the order?

CHAPTER SIXTEEN

The "Close by Contrast"

A false balance is an abomination to the Lord; but a just weight is his delight.
—Proverbs, 11:1.

Don't Try to Sell the Prospect—Help Him to Decide

In my experience with modern sales literature, Hawkins was the first man to point out that the decision to buy or not to buy is a *weighing process.* "When he [the prospect] weighs the ideas in favor of buying," says Hawkins, "in contrast with the lesser weight of the ideas opposed to buying, he decides to buy. . . . If the balance tips the other way, he says No."

John T. A. Ely and Daniel Starch say in their "Salesmanship for Everybody," "Almost invariably, the difficulty in closing arises from the fact that when the prospect signs your order, he must make some offsetting or corresponding sacrifice."

Salesmen blunder in closing because they disregard this fact. They do not take into consideration that because the prospect must make a sacrifice when he buys from you, he is weighing in his mind the advantages of the course you advocate against the advantages of pursuing the course he had in mind when you began your talk.

Many salesmen adopt the policy of presenting only the advantages of the proposition in the close. This policy has its dangers. I recommend that both the advantages and disadvantages be presented.

Once a Buick salesman and a Chrysler salesman were both working on me. But every time the Buick salesman told me the good points of the Buick, I was thinking of the advantages of owning a Chrysler. And every time the Chrysler salesman told me what I would miss if I didn't buy a Chrysler, I was thinking of all the good things I had been told about the Buick.

Neither salesman got both the advantages and disadvantages before me at the same time. So I bought a Studebaker!

Don't Be an Ostrich!

Salesmen say, "It is dangerous at the time of closing to bring up any reasons why the prospect should not buy."

How can it possibly be "dangerous"? You have nothing to lose, because the prospect will bring up the disadvantages anyway; you have a lot to gain, because you can do it fairly—while your prospect might not.

Since it is unsafe to let the prospect do his own weighing, you take over the job for him. You balance the advantages against the disadvantages and show that the advantages of buying from you weigh by far the more.

Suppose, for example, you were trying to sell a public-speaking course, you could say:

"Mr. Prospect, before you make a decision, let's weigh the advantages against the disadvantages. Let's consider the disadvantages first. What are they? Well, first, it will cost you money—$96. Next, it takes time—one or two nights a week for seventeen weeks. Third, it requires courage to stand up and talk. Fourth, it requires effort. It's lots less trouble *not* to take the course. Now, Mr. Prospect, can you think of any other reasons why you should not take the course?"

Generally he can't, so you go on. "Let's look now at the advantages of taking our public-speaking course. It will help you to overcome fear. It will give you poise and self-confidence. It will teach you how to think on your feet. It will put you in a position to earn more money. It will prepare you for advancement.

"Which weighs the more, Mr. Prospect, the advantages or the disadvantages?"

This is a "close by contrast." I don't know whether or not it is a *good* close by contrast. I know, however, that it works, because I have used it successfully on many hundreds of prospects.

The writer recommends to you this Hawkins method of closing.

It works!

Thousands of salesmen under my direction have used it successfully for years.

I ask you to give it a sincere, intelligent, persistent trial. If you do, it will become your standard method of closing.

You Reassure the Prospect

Charles B. Roth, in his excellent book "The Secret of Closing Sales," says: "The closing secret is that you must overcome any fears in your prospect's mind. Before you press for the close, you must reassure him. You must restore his confidence and courage."

This is exactly what is done in the closing-by-contrast

method, when you end by giving all the reasons why the prospect should buy. You say to him, in effect: "Mr. Prospect, I
have given you all the reasons why you should not buy, and
I have given you all the reasons why you should buy; and I
have shown you that there are more and stronger reasons for
buying than there are for not buying."

In other words, you are reassuring him; you are restoring
his confidence in his own judgment; you are making it easier
for him to sign.

Put the Prospect Out of His Suffering

By listing the advantages and disadvantages of buying you
not only *reassure* the prospect but you often relieve him of
the torment of indecision.

Exide News says:

In helping a customer to make up his mind, it probably will be
good salesmanship to recognize his mental discomfort and some of
the possible causes of it. For instance, Mr. Smith knows he needs
a new battery and the thoughts that may be passing through his mind
might be like this:

"I didn't expect to have to buy a battery this week—wanted to
buy that new fishing reel—confound it! My insurance is due and
Sarah wants those new drapes—what would happen if I bought a
cheap battery?—better not—maybe it wouldn't stand up—wonder
if this fellow's telling me the truth?—this one costs a couple of dollars more than this cheap one—don't think there's a bit of difference
in those two batteries—maybe there is—wonder if I can squeeze the
money out for that new fishing reel?—can't do it this pay. . . ."

And on and on the stream of thought flows through the customer's
mind until something happens to break it off and force a decision.
And what a relief when the decision is made!

You make it easy for him to make the decision, and to get out of his mental torment, by placing in front of him the reasons for buying and the reasons against buying and showing him that the reasons in favor of buying weigh the heavier.

Some Suggestions on Closing

Here is what we learned, through years of use, about this technique of closing:

Don't let the prospect do his own weighing. Arguments that are floating around in a man's head are hard for him to measure. Richard C. Borden and Alvin C. Busse, in their excellent book, "How to Win an Argument," say:

"[In a sales argument] *encourage* your opponent to continue speaking. . . . It leads your opponent to deflate automatically any 'hobgoblin' points at the back of his mind, which loom large there merely because they are hazy and blurred—because they have never been put into words before and thus brought into the light for logical scrutiny. Verbal expression is a cruel clarifier. . . . A point your opponent has expressed is less dangerous to you than one he has not expressed."

Just the other day I was trying to sell a sales manager a course in selling for his men. He started in on what he assumed was a strong argument. As so often happens, the longer the talk, the weaker the argument became. Finally he said ruefully, "I guess I'd better stop. Now that I get my argument out in the open, it's more in your favor than it is in mine."

Since you cannot, in the closing stages of the sale, get your opponent to voice his reasons against buying, you bring them out in the open for him.

Since decision is a weighing process and since you are more likely to do the weighing fairly than your prospect is, you *must* take the job out of his hands and do it yourself.

You Must Know How to Weigh

Here are some rules that answer your question, "How can I weigh effectively?"

1. Talk with courage and confidence. Unless you sound as though you thought the ideas in favor of buying weigh heavier than those against buying, you can't hope that your prospect will believe it. The prospect really desires to buy but he has not too much confidence in his own judgment. He fears to make a mistake. He wants you to confirm his hopes and desires.

2. Don't slur over this summary of the advantages of your product on the ground that you have already been over them in detail. Don't say too much about the advantages but say what you do say forcefully.

3. Let your attitude be, not that you are going to strong-arm your prospect into signing an order for something he really does not want, but rather that you are going to present him with the facts and reasons for and against buying, *so that he can make up his own mind.*

Give Yourself a Break!

Hawkins gives these suggestions for making the points in your favor seem heavier than the points against you:

Make the ideas against buying seem trivial by using tones and gestures that suggest lightness. "Of course this is the most expensive washer on the market." "Yes, it calls for quite an expenditure to put in this installation." The words are against you, the tones and the gestures can be for you!

Naturally, in the same way, you try to make the ideas in your favor seem important by tone and gestures that suggest weight and importance. "It pays for itself through savings" can be said in a tone and with gestures that make it weigh an ounce—or a ton!

Show that there are many more ideas in favor of buying than against it.

Yes, but suppose there are more ideas *against* buying.

Well, we know that a two-pound bag of sugar looks lighter than two one-pound bags. So, if a salesman must deal with too many No ideas, he puts two or three in one package. In other words, he combines them. "Of course I know your secretary will not like a dictating machine at first and it will take her a little time to shave records and there is the off chance that a cylinder will be broken." Three objections combined in one. Certainly they do not sound so weighty as though the three had been presented separately.

Make the ideas in favor of buying attractive, those against buying unattractive. How? For example: "I know your secretary will object, but then, at $50 a week, you are paying her to do what you ask—not what she likes." You have tried to make that objection unattractive. Now for the other side: "This machine will actually save you an hour a day. You have every right to spend that saved hour on the golf course, piling up health for yourself." Note that you have painted this in bright colors.

Don't hurry the summing up of the points of advantage of
your product. Pause after each one to let it sink in. Some
salesmen end the summing up of each important point with
a question that calls for an answer of Yes: "Earnings like
that ought to assure you regular dividends, oughtn't they?"
"$25,000 ought to be enough to pay for the education of your
children, oughtn't it?"

Don't Skip Any Contrary Points

Don't make the mistake of leaving out any of the points
against you. Not only is it bad sportsmanship, it is worse
salesmanship! If your prospect catches you leaving out
one point he will rightly wonder how many more points you
are leaving out. Once he feels that you are weighing unfairly,
you may as well fold up your scales and move on to the next
prospect.

Don't be afraid of the points against you, and especially
don't try to keep them a secret from your prospect. They are
in his head now. And since they are, you will be better off
to get them out of his head and on the table in front of you.
Don't let your prospect think you are trying to make him forget some point in favor of your competitor, or he will mag-
nify it—perhaps to a point where it will cost you the order.

Before you start presenting the negative side, it is an advantage to find out the chief objection—to find out what the
prospect considers the largest sacrifice he must make to buy
your goods.

If you have asked plenty of questions and if you have
thought of the problem all along from his viewpoint, you
probably know already your highest hurdle. If you don't,

some authorities recommend that before you try to close, you ask your prospect, point blank, "What is your chief objection to buying?" I've never tried it but I feel that it ought to work. A spoken objection is always less dangerous than an unspoken objection.

Note the Advantages of Knowing How to Close

Look at the advantages of having a time-tested closing technique and of knowing how to use it. Instead of finding yourself, right at the moment of closing, with no idea in the world what you are going to say, you know exactly what you are going to say. You are going to compare the advantages of doing what you suggest with the advantages of pursuing the alternative course the prospect has in mind. You are going to do it in such a way as to convince your prospect that your plan weighs heavier in the balance than the other one.

You compare the advantages of buying the Buick you sell with the Chrysler that your prospect has looked at. You weigh the advantages of buying a cash register with the disadvantages of having no record of sales. You point out the advantages of using dictating machines compared with the present plan of depending on shorthand.

Face It, Lads, Face It!

Lots of salesmen make heavy going of this matter of pointing out the reasons for *not* buying their product. Maybe you will.

"I don't know any reason why people shouldn't buy my product," you say.

Does everybody buy it? Of course not. So there must be reasons for not buying it—and you'd better hurry and find out what the reasons are!

The salesman who can't think of any reasons for not buying his product suffers from one of the worst selling weaknesses— an inability to think of the selling problem from his prospect's side.

Remember, the prospect has been thinking of his reasons for not buying all the way through the sales talk. The more he thinks about them, the larger and more important they become.

The best way to deflate them—to bring them down to their real size—is to state them. Don't be afraid to do it—it makes sales.

You Will Gradually Develop Some Standard Closers

Note another advantage. This close can be standardized to a considerable extent. You cannot have one grand list of advantages that will fit all prospects. You can, however, have a list for each important group. For example, let's say you are selling washing machines. One group of women send their clothes to the laundry. Your job in selling any individual in this group is to compare the advantages of washing at home with those of sending clothes to the laundry. You will use substantially the same list for all women in that group. Another group do their washing the old-fashioned way. One list of advantages will be equally applicable to virtually all women in this list. Some women are using competing machines. One list of advantages will do for them. Some are using an old model of your make. Another list for them.

"A lot of lists," you say. True. But not nearly as many as though you made up a new one for each prospect.

If the prospect admits that he needs what you are selling, that your goods are right, that the company which makes them is satisfactory, that the price is right, and that he ought to buy now—then he has *bought,* and he must be made to realize it.

CHAPTER SEVENTEEN

Get the Order on a "Minor Point"

To become a champion, fight one more round.
—JAMES J. CORBETT.

All right—you have finished the weighing process. Your prospect sees that the advantages of buying your product vastly out-weigh the disadvantages.

But the prospect probably does not say, "All right, wrap it up."

No, he probably sits there, awaiting your next move.

Shall you ask him, "Well, will you buy or won't you?" Such a challenge would be better than to say nothing. But better still, close on a minor point or an alternative proposal ("double question").

Why?

Because any man hates to say, "I'm whipped—I give up."

An excellent example of the human reluctance to admit defeat was given by Henry W. Grady in his speech, "The New South," when he said: "Or the soldier returning home after the surrender and roasting some corn by the roadside, who made the remark to his comrades, 'You may leave the South if you want to but I'm going back to Sandersville, kiss my wife, and raise a crop; and if the Yankees fool with me again I'll whip them again.' "

Further along in the same speech, Grady said: "When Lee

surrendered—I don't say when Johnson surrendered—because I understand he still alludes to the time he met General Sherman last as the time when he 'determined to abandon any further prosecution of the struggle'—when Lee surrendered, I say, and when Johnson quit. . . ."

In other words, they just naturally hated to admit defeat—and so does your prospect.

Your prospect probably struggled against being interested. He put up objection after objection through the conviction part of your sales talk. He fought against desire. He hated to admit that the reasons in favor of buying weighed more than those against buying. He has given ground reluctantly, fighting every step of the way.

Do you expect him now to wave the white flag voluntarily? He's whipped and he knows it. But he hates to admit it.

If you are wise you will let him save face.

You will do it by assuming that of course he has decided for himself that he is going to buy and that the only decision is on some minor point—or between two proposals. By assuming that he has decided to buy, you dodge the implication that you are making him decide.

Here Are Some Questions That Get the Orders

If you should say to him, "Well, you've got to admit that I've made you buy," you know what the answer would be. No, instead you assume that he has made the decision for himself and that he is now weighing in his mind some minor decision, so you ask him, for instance: "Which carriage do you prefer, the wide or the narrow?" You assume that of course he is going to buy the machines and that the only question is as to the width of the carriage. If he says "narrow" or "wide," you hand him the order blank. Here are some suggested minor points or double questions that you can use in closing:

"Which base do you like better—the high or the low?"

"Would you rather take the cash discount, or do you like the payment plan better?"

"Which of these do you prefer, this one or that one?"

"Would you like delivery this week end, or will Monday be all right?"

"How do you prefer paying, weekly or monthly?"

"Where do you plan using it, here or there?"

"Would you pay by cash or by check?"

"Will this cord be long enough for your use, or shall I have the shop lengthen it?"

"Would you have it delivered to the office or the house?"

"Which finish do you prefer, walnut or mahogany?"

"What signature do you want on the advertising matter we give you?"

Realsilk salesmen use three trial closes, based on (a) color, (b) on how many pairs, and (c) on delivery date.

How to Find Out Whether or Not This Is a Trick

Some salesmen seem to look on this minor point closing as a trick—a clever way to take advantage of the prospect.

I remember that I once suggested this plan of closing to an old-time securities salesman. He was horrified. "Why," said he, "it's not ethical—it's a trick."

The best way to convince yourself that it is no trick is to

try to use it to close somebody who is not sold. Under those circumstances it will never work.

Unless the prospect really wants to buy, unless he is convinced, unless his desire is aroused, unless he realizes that the advantages outweigh the disadvantages—unless he sees that the purchase will really benefit him—no closing tactics on earth will get the order.

So have no fear of the ethics of closing on a minor point.

It is no trick. In fact, it works only when you are doing the prospect a favor by using it.

This technique of assuming that of course the prospect is going to buy is not new. Ben Franklin used it in a pamphlet he wrote to help Robert Grace sell the stoves that Grace manufactured on Franklin's model.

In this pamphlet, Franklin pointed out (not too truthfully) that open fireplaces caused many women to lose their teeth ". . . and do also very much contribute to damage the eyes, shrivel the skin, and bring on early the appearances of old age." Carl Van Doren, in his "Benjamin Franklin," goes on to say, "Having artfully appealed to women, Franklin went on to explain . . . how Pennsylvania fireplaces were constructed. Then, one by one, he gave fourteen advantages and answered the objections that had been raised. After this, as his argument was complete and unanswerable, he directed workmen how to install the new stoves."

Make It Easy for Them to Say Yes

Some excellent suggestions for ways of asking the final decisive questions are suggested by Wilfrid D. Galpin of the

General Electric Co. in his pamphlet "Twenty-five Ways to Close the Sale." To sum them up:

(a) **The Subtle Question.** Ask a question that will enable the prospect to indicate that already in his own mind he is enjoying the ownership of the article. For example: "I can just see your family enjoying those delicious frozen deserts you are going to give them next Sunday—can't you?"

If he can see his family enjoying one of the benefits of a modern mechanical refrigerator, he has bought one!

(b) **The Instruction Close.** In this case, you ask the prospect if he would like to know how to use the article—then start in at once giving him instructions. If he shows interest, he is ready for the order blank.

(c) **The Name-spelling Close.** When your order blank is out, ask the prospect how his name is spelled, what his initials are, or what his street address is. If he lets you write these facts on the order blank, he is sold.

(d) **The Action Close.** (This close was designed for selling electric refrigerators—maybe it would work in your line too.) The salesman says something like this: "The G-E refrigerator is strong as a safe." Then he slams the door as hard as he can three or four times. If the prospect stops the salesman, she is sold. She already considers that it is *her* refrigerator he is abusing—and the signing of the order follows easily.

CHAPTER EIGHTEEN

Some General Rules for Closing

You believe easily what you hope for earnestly.
—TERENCE.

Rule 1: You should always expect to make the sale. From J. C. Aspley's excellent "Closing the Sale" I take this incident:

A highly successful salesmanager, a man who is now general manager of his company, was asked by a beginner how he could tell when it was time to close. . . .

The old-timer's reply was a classic. Said he: "Don't wait until you get to him, sell him on the way. Simply go to get the order signed."

Be determined to sell your prospect. The will to sell puts over many hard sales.

Did you ever see a tomcat fight his way out of a corner? On the way out he will whip three dogs, each three times his size —and he will do it on sheer determination. He has made up his mind to get out of that corner—and out he goes. If the dogs get in his way, that's their fault.

"How can I believe I am going to make the next sale," you ask, "when I haven't closed an order for three days?"

The answer is, you can believe anything you want to. You can have faith—and "Faith," says Mark Twain, "is believing what you know ain't so."

George Hopkins used to tell his salesmen to say over and over again to themselves before they made a call, "I'm going to sell this man—I *know* I am."

Unless you expect to make the sale, you cut your chances of closing almost to zero.

Rule 2: Make it harder for the prospect to turn him down than to sign the order blank. You do this in the desire step of the selling process suggested in this book. You point out your prospect's want of what you are selling, you show that your article will supply this want, you paint a word picture of his satisfaction as a result of owning it, you weigh the advantages against the disadvantages and show that the advantages weigh more. Certainly you are making it hard for the prospect to say, "I lack it, your product will supply the lack, I'd certainly enjoy owning it, the advantages vastly outweigh the disadvantages—but still I'm not going to buy it."

If Your Thinking Is Right, Your Poise Will Be Right

Rule 3: Don't wobble! If the salesman sways mentally at the time of closing, he shouldn't be surprised if the prospect sways too. Be poised, calm, and decisive at the moment of closing. You should find no trouble in being so if you are not thinking about yourself but instead are thinking about the prospect and his needs and how your goods will satisfy his lack.

Rule 4: Ask for the order. In "The Salesman's Refrigerator Primer" of the General Electric Company—an able document, made especially interesting by the fact that it contains twenty-five different methods of closing—Wilfrid D. Galpin says:

Not long ago the fact was impressed on a group of salesmen at their regular morning meeting that they should not be afraid to ask for the order and to keep on asking for the order. After the meeting, about noon of the same day, one of the best men in the group came into the show room, proudly waving an order. It appeared that as a result of the meeting, he went out to see one of his prospects, Mrs. Johnson, and said, "I've been out here four or five times to see you and I've told you all about the proposition, so I've come out this morning to ask you for the order." "I know," she replied, "I've been trying to give you the order, but you wanted me to have a demonstration. My sister has one of them and I know all about it." Would you believe it? Because he thought she had to have a demonstration, he had never even asked for the order.

This Calls for Faith

Rule 5: You should not only *think* that you are going to get the order but you should also *feel* and *look* as though you expected to get it. The tone of your voice should convey the same idea. Unless you can believe that the prospect ought to buy, unless you can believe he is going to buy, you will never make many sales.

Rule 6: Keep one strong point about your product or proposition in reserve for use in case your prospect balks just at the point of closing.

This is important. The expert salesman is never caught at the close of the sale without one good closing point held in reserve—ready to use to clinch the deal.

The automobile salesman says, "On this job, I can let you have white-walled tires without extra cost." Servel salesmen are instructed to say, "Note the double-action door handle.

You can open it easily with your arms full—just by touching it with your arm."

Don't Quit Too Readily

Rule 7: Never leave a prospect until he has said No at least seven times.

Columbus heard No for eighteen years before he got the money and the ships that carried him to the New World.

No matter how hard the turndowns or how firm the refusal, ask for the order once more just before you leave. Roth reports that one company that adopted this rule as company policy increased their sales by 25 per cent.

Rule 8: Don't be too tense in this step of the sale. Don't act as though it were the last minute of the last round of a championship fight—as though you had to knock out your opponent with one final desperate rain of punches. Your tenseness will warn the prospect.

Rule 9: Don't debate. If your prospect wants to argue, then you are away ahead of yourself in starting to close. Go back and start in to tell him some of the things that your goods will do for him.

Rule 10: While the prospect is signing, *you talk*. Don't say anything important—but don't let a dead silence ensue. It may give the prospect a chance to think up another objection. Talk steadily about the advantages of your product or service —so he will not have time to think up any new reason for not buying.

Rule 11: Don't let your mind wander. It is dangerous at any stage of the sale, fatal in closing. If for just one second your mind strays off to a golf date, a girl date, a new job, or an old mother-in-law, you may as well pack up and depart. Don't think of the next prospect—one sale at a time, please. Especially, don't think about what you are going to make out of this sale. If you think only about the service you can render the prospect, your brain will not get you into one bit of trouble.

"I Don't Want Any—What Do You Sell?"

Rule 12: Don't expect people to *want* what you sell, just because they *need* it. J. C. Aspley tells of the salesman who was selling Babbitt's Cleanser and who was told by every dealer he called on that Pyle's Pearline had the call. Finally, just to get himself in the right mental attitude, he would go into a store and say merely, "Pyle's Pearline"—and let the grocer assume he was representing Pyle's. He found, as he had suspected, that when grocers thought he was from Pyle's, they began telling him at once that Babbitt's was the only cleanser demanded by their trade.

The moral: Whatever you sell—they don't want it.

Rule 13: Talk "profits" to dealers. E. G. Weir, who sold so many Round Oak stoves that he was made an executive, said: "Translate the thing you are selling into terms of profits and prestige for the buyer. . . . [The words] 'Profits today that you never dreamed of' never failed me. . . . 'Profits' and 'prestige' are magic words. . . . The further you go, the better they sound."

Rule 14: Don't let your prospect have anything to look at or fiddle with while you are closing. You want all his attention. So gather up your exhibits, catalogues, and circulars and get them out of sight before you begin to close.

Don't Let Yourself Be Put Off

Rule 15: Never agree to call back on a prospect until you have tried every known way of closing on the spot—and failed. Every time you let a prospect put you off, you are weaker in the eyes of two important people—the prospect and yourself. If a prospect promises to buy later and gives no good reason for the postponement, either he is not telling the truth or he could be sold *now*.

Don't be put off—it costs time and orders.

Remember also that between your call and your call-back, your competitor may slip in and get the order.

Rule 16: Save up one good strong question for the final push. The Equitable recommends these questions to its agents:

"You realize that you ought to have this protection, don't you?"

"Hadn't you just as well settle this matter now?"

"Why delay in doing now what you admit is a duty to your loved ones?"

"If you knew you couldn't get this protection next month, you would take it now, wouldn't you?" (Wait until he answers Yes.) "Then why run the risk of not getting it at all?"

Rule 17: Use any legitimate "hurry-ups." It is hardly necessary to tell a salesman to use any valid reasons that may exist for buying now. If the price is going up, if the offer is to be withdrawn, if the supply is running low, you will of course use such a point to encourage a prompt decision.

You Can Close with an Example

Rule 18: Use an example (or "for instance") to give the final push. In other words, cite a case that is analogous to the case of your prospect.

I recall once, after I had spoken at a meeting to promote a Dale Carnegie public-speaking class, a young man came up and said that he could not decide whether or not to take the course. I asked him a few questions. Then I said, "Let me tell you the case of a young man who faced about the same problem that you now face. Like yourself, he was trying to become a salesman, and like yourself, he was having no success." Then I told him in considerable detail how this man had taken the course—and that while it was in progress he had forced his way into the lead of his sales force. I told how within two years he was made district sales manager of his organization.

Other people crowded up and I had to end my sales talk at the end of the example. But I was gratified to see the young man to whom I had been talking walk over to the enrollment table and make out his check.

Get the Order Blank Out Early

Rule 19. Even after you have your prospect's agreement to buy, in some forms of selling you have the additional hurdle of getting the order blank signed and, in some even more trying cases (like securities), of getting the payment in full.

I never could believe very enthusiastically in the necessity

of using suggestion, hypnotism, or force in getting the pen
into the prospect's hands. If he has gone through the other
steps, he is not likely to back away from signing.

Here are some practical suggestions:

(*a*) If you use an order blank, bring it out early. It often
pays to have terms or conditions printed on it, so that you
will have a pretext to hand it to the prospect even before you
expect him to sign it.

(*b*) Once you have it out, *leave it out*—so that the prospect will get used to seeing it.

(*c*) Write something on the order blank before you hand
it to your customer—your own name or the prospect's address. If you have done this, the prospect is more likely to
sign.

High Pressure in Kansas

Miss Zelda Gordon of Augusta, Kansas, who acted as a
temporary secretary for me in Oklahoma City while this book
was being revised, told me this story:

A magazine salesman approached me one day with a deal for three
monthly magazines. He pulled out a contract and asked my name
and address. When I told him, he filled out the contract. Before I
knew what it was all about or had said that I would accept the offer,
he handed the contract over to me to sign. Because I did not know
anything about contracts and because I did not know for sure that
I could refuse to sign a contract after it was made out, I signed it.
The salesman made me feel that since I had let him fill out one of
his contract blanks, I had to sign it.

Roth calls this "the physical-action technique." He says,
in brief, that you should do something, like filling out an
order blank—something that the customer must either stop

you from doing or else leave himself in a position where he has almost a moral obligation to sign.

This seems to me to be high pressure. It is a form of taking the decision away from the buyer. Personally, I would not use it.

Don't say, "Sign here." Men have for years built up a resistance to "signing here."

Instead say, as security salesmen and insurance salesmen do, "Put your name here just as you wish it to appear on the [certificate or policy]." Or "Write your name here as I have written it above," or "Sign your name as you usually do."

Other possible ways of asking for the signature are "Just your name and address, please"; "Now if you will just initial this, please."

"How Do You Ask for the Money?" Just Ask!

And now, how do you ask for the money? Literally hundreds of salesmen have asked me that question.

The best way I know to ask for the money is to *ask for it.* At this late stage in the sale, why hesitate to ask? You might say, as we did in the security business: "If you will give me your check now, I'll attach it to the order and see that it goes through promptly." Or you could say: "I'll fill out the order while you write your check." Or "Please make the check out to the company. The amount is $ . . ."

Rule 20: Don't let down at the end.

CHAPTER NINETEEN

If You Are Turned Down, What?

"What do I do," you ask, "if I go all the way through my selling talk and then get a clear-cut and emphatic No?"

Here indeed is a hard question to answer.

You need not worry about the Noes you get on your trial closes. You just disregard them. But now, at the end of the last step, your prospect says, "No, I don't want to buy."

What then?

POINT ONE: *Don't quit.* If you have asked your prospect a lot of questions, if you have smoked out his objections, you have found out long before the closing step whether or not you are in a hopeless sales situation. Once in a very great while, your prospect will hold his one unanswerable objection for the very end of his sales talk. In general, however, he will shoot it at you far earlier than that. So, if you get a turn-down at the end, it is probably a sign, not that your prospect does not want your goods, but rather that you have failed in your sales talk.

So you go right on trying to sell him.

Many wars have been won by a series of lost battles—our own Revolution, for example. Read John Marshall's "Life of George Washington" if you want to see clearly how a series of apparently conclusive Noes can be turned into a grand final Yes. If you read Marshall's book you will conclude, no doubt, that the reason our troops were so often barefoot was

164

that they wore out their shoes running away! Yet in the end they won the war.

A lesson from 1776 for timorous salesmen!

POINT TWO: *Always prepare in advance for a flat turndown.* Before you call on a man say to yourself, "If he tries to turn me down, here's what I am going to do and say." Don't prepare to retreat—prepare to attack from a new and previously selected position.

POINT THREE: *Try to determine* why *your prospect has said No.* The chances are it is not the goods, it is not the prospect, it is *you.*

Why do people refuse to buy something they really lack and want and can afford? Often it is indecision, even more often it is fear.

If the salesman correctly diagnoses the complaint, the cure is usually relatively easy.

The curing of indecision will be taken up under Put-offs, in Chapters XXII and XXIII.

If the resistance is not due to indecision but to fear, it is necessary first to answer the question, "Fear of what?" If it is fear of spending the money, then the salesman goes back and shows that it really does not cost money to buy—or that the prospect is spending the money anyway, even if he does not buy. If it is fear that the goods are not what the salesman claims, then—assuming that the salesman knows his facts— the cure depends on the exact nature of the disease.

A husband's fear that his wife will not approve is often hard to combat. Once a retired wealthy and not overly bright man strolled to town through the bitter cold of a Maine winter, went to the meat market, looked over the stock of meat, bought some pork, and departed. In half an hour he came back and threw the pork down on the counter with these words, "She don't like pork."

In general, if the salesman will show the prospect that the person who may object will profit by the transaction, the objection may be overcome. But a wife's objection to something her husband wants to buy is hard to overcome. When possible, sell the wife too.

Naturally, the best way to find out why the prospect has turned you down is to *ask*. The question, "Why have you decided not to buy it, Mr. Blank?" is likely to elicit an answer that will help you to carry on.

Don't hesitate to ask. The prospect has listened to your sales talk. You have shown clearly that you consider it to his advantage to buy. If he turns you down, what is more natural than to ask, "Why?"

Be sure not to show any feeling because of the turn-down, other than surprise. Don't seem disappointed. Don't show anger or fear. You are curious to know why any reasonable man should turn down such a reasonable proposal, so you ask, "Why?"

POINT FOUR: *Disarm your prospect.*

What do I mean by that?

I mean that your prospect has not only said no but at your request has also probably told you why he has said No.

If you started in to argue with him you would meet with a man who had dug in and was prepared to resist forever.

How can you get his mind off his refusal? How can you get him into a state of mind where he is willing to listen to some more sales talk?

Here are some effective plans:

Plan A: Pretend that you have given up. Get up, gather up

your materials, talk about the weather or some neutral and harmless subject. Ask the way to your next prospect. Then suddenly, with your hand on the door, fire at your prospect some telling question or some strong selling point you have held in reserve for that moment.

Plan B: Accuse yourself. Say, "I must be a poor salesman. I ought to go back to peddling ice. If I weren't one of the worst salesmen in the world," etc. Pile it on *thick.* Try to go after yourself so hard that your prospect will come to your rescue.

Then, without warning, go back into a summary of the advantages to him of buying your product.

Plan C: Throw yourself on your prospect's mercy.

Ask the prospect what mistake you made, why you failed, what you might do to improve your sales talk, how you could have gone about the talk so that it would have brought in the order.

Be entirely sincere about this. If you are, your prospect will probably give you some good ideas. He may change his mind and buy—may actually sell himself.

All right, you have so handled the situation that your prospect has let down his fists, relaxed his hands, and is ready to listen again—*if you have something worth saying.*

Plan D: Make a strong close. Yes, but what?

Naturally, what you say will depend on the answer your prospect gave when you asked him why he was not willing to buy. You may have convinced him. Perhaps you did not answer one of his serious objections. Perhaps you did not arouse his desire. Perhaps he does not realize his lack of your article or service. Possibly, when you weighed the advantages and disadvantages, you did not make the advantages of buying seem to weigh more.

If your prospect has given his real reason for not buying, then you know exactly what to say—I hope.

But suppose he refuses, or evades the point.

Often this is a good time to ask some more questions. Check each point:

Interest: "Do you feel, Mr. Jones, that this machine really will save you $100 a year?"

Conviction: "Have I satisfied you that this machine will move xy cubic yards of earth a day?"

Desire: "Are you dissatisfied with the way your gas oven bakes?"

The answers to such questions are quite likely to tell you what to say next.

Make His Refusal Seem Absurd

In "The Knack of Selling More," Burton Bigelow suggests the plan of carrying the prospect's No to absurdity. If a salesman applied this technique to say the Kitchen-Aid, he might say something like this:

You have just said, "No, I'm not going to buy one today." I know what that means to you, but have you ever thought of what it means to your wife? It means that a lot of work that can be done better and cheaper with an electric motor will have to be done by your wife—at the expense of her health and strength. You are saying that you don't care if she has to beat cakes by hand. You are saying that she can blister her hands on that old-fashioned coffee grinder. You are making it clear that if she wants homemade ice cream, she has to bend over the freezer and turn the crank herself—a back-breaking job, as you well know. Mr. Blank, I can't believe you mean just this. Surely you realize that a few dollars down and a small monthly payment is little, compared with saving the health and strength of your wife. If you pay $—— down, I'll leave the machine and it will begin saving labor for your wife today.

In other words, the salesman summed up the disadvantages that will result from not buying. He made it seem absurd not to buy!

The Burroughs Adding Machine Company recommends these sentences for use on the hesitant prospect:

"A thing worth having is worth having now."

"The sooner you get it, the sooner it will start saving money for you."

"Putting it off is like paying more for it. Decide now, when it will cost you least."

"The facts are clearer now than they will be again. There is every reason why you should decide now."

If you habitually accept Noes, you're no salesman—and never will be.

In the insurance business it has long been recommended that when a prospect says, "I don't want life insurance," you reply, "Of course you don't. If you did, I'd be too late. But do you know *why* you don't want it?"

If the turndown is backed up with what appears a valid reason for not buying, try to see if you can't save something. I was calling with L. G. Nichols, of the Dale Carnegie Institute, in an effort to sell a sales course to a company that employed thirty or forty salesmen. The sales manager turned us down because all his regular salesmen were then taking a competing course. Mr. Nichols, a former insurance salesman, urged the sales manager to put into our course two or three young men who were being prepared for selling jobs. He suggested to the sales manager that this was the best plan for finding out whether or not our course was any good. Thus he saved a few enrollments out of what had looked to me like a total loss.

CHAPTER TWENTY

A Sum-up of the Closing Rules

Which of the rules for closing are vitally important?
These:

1. Expect to close. If you don't expect to close, you won't close very often.

2. Use trial closes all the way through your talk. Then you will be sure to start closing in time.

3. Close by comparing the reasons for not buying with the reasons in favor of buying. The prospect will do it anyway— you can do it better.

4. Ask for the order on a minor point or an alternative proposal. Don't ask the prospect whether he is going to buy. Assume that of course he is going to buy and ask him if he wants the green or the brown, if he wants it delivered today or next week.

5. Always save one strong point for the final push at the end.

6. Don't quit until the prospect has said No at least seven times—or has thrown you out!

Maxims

"Faith may be defined briefly as an illogical belief in the occurrence of the improbable."—H. L. MENCKEN.

The best way to get a Yes is to expect a Yes.

Think one step ahead of your prospect. Then you are waiting for him at the close—and are in a stronger position to lead him along to the signature. If he thinks a lap ahead of you—you're distanced.

"They are able to close because they think they are able to close."—VIRGIL (once removed).

Do you float or sink? Are you buoyant or waterlogged? When you are knocked under water by an objection or a refusal, unless you can bob up as a cork bobs up when it is pushed under water, you will never be much of a salesman. How do you rebound?

If the prospect buys, compliment him sincerely on his good judgment.

A good salesman may pick up his order book a half-dozen times in the course of a sale and start to pass it to his prospect. If the prospect doesn't reach for it, start selling him again.

CHAPTER TWENTY-ONE

How to Answer Objections

*A man who will not kick on price is not very much interested.
He must be interested or he wouldn't kick.*

—JOSEPH E. ROGERS.

When the average man thinks seriously about buying some
article or service (other than a routine item like flour or
coffee) he thinks at once of reasons for not buying. This is
likely to be true even if he desires to buy and has practically
made up his mind to buy.

To understand objections and why they are raised, consider
your own case. Suppose you had been getting along with a
slightly battered Chevrolet, and suppose your earnings are
good and you have the money to buy a better car. Then suppose a Buick salesman calls, demonstrates his car, and starts
in on a sales talk.

What is happening in your mind? Probably it is seething.
You are saying to yourself, "Shucks, I don't need a new car.
I'm getting along all right with the old one. It's foolish to
spend this money right now—I might need it sometime. . . .
On the other hand, my car is getting pretty old. It may not be
safe. It has old-fashioned glass, which might cut us danger-
ously in an accident. . . . Then again, why should I buy a
Buick? The Chrysler looks pretty good to me. . . . Of course,
I like to stick along with General Motors. . . . Still, Chrys-

ler has a mighty live organization. . . . I wonder what my wife will think? She's not so hot for spending money . . . ," and so on.

Is it not natural, with such thoughts running through your mind, that you should raise objections, should try to put off making the decision, even though you really want to buy?

You need a new car. You have practically decided to buy one. Still you are reluctant to make the decision. You want someone to prove to you that today is the day to buy—that the Buick is the car. So naturally your mental steam pressure escapes through the safety valve of such remarks as, "I have no money," "I like the brake on the Chrysler better," "I want to talk it over with my wife."

These remarks may be true objections or they may be mere put-offs.

It is well to recognize that put-offs (such as "I want to think it over"—"Come back next week") are normally the result of indecision, of a reluctance or inability on the part of the prospect to make up his mind. Yet a put-off is not always a sign of indecision. When your prospect says, "I want to think it over," it may mean that he doesn't like what you are offering and would not consider buying it. He has simply tried to spare your feelings.

The Same Words May Have Different Meanings

On the other hand, a true objection (for example, "I would not buy an over-the-counter stock") may indicate any one of a variety of states of mind on the part of your prospect. It may be

1. A trivial objection, just thrown in to make conversation.

2. A half-baked objection—something the prospect read or heard somewhere, brought up largely to impress the salesman that the prospect is a pretty smart buyer and knows a thing or two.

Selling Magazine says: "In a good many of your sales calls, there is an even chance that your prospect doesn't believe a single thing he says against your proposition. He simply has elected to match his wits with yours, and he doesn't care who wins so long as a good scrap is enjoyed by all."

3. A genuine objection—something that the prospect considers as a real reason for not buying.

Are objections of this kind unavoidable? As a practical matter, yes. However, you can lessen their number. How? (*a*) By telling the complete story and (*b*) by being sure that your story has been told clearly.

4. An indication of indecision on the part of your prospect. Instead of saying, "I want to think it over," he hopes to postpone the decision by bringing up some objection.

So here is a good general rule for handling objections: *Try to understand what is going on in your prospect's mind.* If you know what he is thinking about your goods and why he is thinking it, you are in a better position to answer objections and to close the sale. And the way to know what he is thinking is to ask a lot of questions.

What Is Your Prospect Thinking?

Once I was out making sales calls with a security salesman. When the talk was about over, the prospect said, "I have no money."

The salesman was fortunately paying more attention to

what the prospect was *thinking* than to what he was *saying*, so he answered, "How would it be, Mr. Blank, if I came to your house tonight and told your wife about it?"

The prospect agreed and the sale was made—after the wife was sold.

The prospect wanted to buy but he wanted his wife's approval—and he was ashamed to admit it. If the salesman had not guessed what was going on in the prospect's mind, he would not have made the sale.

If you recognize that objections are ordinarily the natural result of mental uncertainty, you will not be terrified by them and you will know better how to handle them successfully.

As D. R. Freeman, once director of sales training for Henry L. Doherty and Company, used to put it: "Objections are as much a part of the selling process as hurdles are part of a hurdle race. When you go into a hurdle race you expect to jump hurdles; when you attempt to make a sale you expect to answer objections."

To the good salesman, most objections are welcome. Your prospect has shown an interest. Why shouldn't you be pleased!

If a prospect "yes-yesses" you all the way through a sales talk and raises no objections, you can generally make up your mind that he is doing it just to be pleasant. He will usually end by turning you down pleasantly but firmly. The fact that he does not think of any objections is an indication, in many cases, that he is not seriously thinking of your offer at all.

If, on the other hand, the prospect does raise many objections, it is strong evidence that he is thinking seriously of buying.

Note this point: an objection is often a question in disguise. When a prospect says, "I don't believe I could ever learn to use a dictating machine," he may really mean, "Do you think I could learn to use a dictating machine?"

Therefore treat most objections not as invitations to argue but as requests for more information.

To answer objections effectively you must

1. Know why prospects raise objections.

2. Know the various kinds of objections, since different sorts of objections must be answered in different ways.

3. Know *when* to answer them.

4. Know *how* to answer them—what to say.

5. Know how to get in the right mental attitude toward both the objection and the objector.

Objections may be broadly classified as follows:

I. Hopeless objections—those that *cannot*, as a matter of practical selling, be answered.

II. Objections that *can* be satisfactorily answered.

I. The Hopeless Objections

If you talk with a man about buying a car and he tells you that he has just gone into bankruptcy and has no money, his objection is valid—and, for the moment at least, unanswerable. This is only one of many unanswerable objections.

A well-to-do woman told me once, "I promised my father forty years ago that I would never buy a share of stock. I have lived up to that promise for forty years—I expect to keep it the rest of my life." That was a valid and a virtually unanswerable objection.

I have often heard security salesmen say, "I am going to

sell that man if it takes the rest of my life." If the prospect in question is a man of great means and a buyer on a large scale, then the ambition is laudable. But in most cases it is a waste of time to batter against the hopeless prospect. The world is full of good prospects who are ready to buy. Therefore do not waste too much time on the hopeless prospect. You might get much personal satisfaction out of sticking to one prospect for ten years and then selling him a small order—but you would have little to show for your efforts.

Calls on prospects who floor you with unanswerable objections need not always be a total loss. Always ask the person who refuses to buy your goods if he does not know somebody who *will* buy them. Good prospects are often suggested by poor prospects.

II. Objections That Can Be Answered

The answerable objections, which constitute an overwhelming proportion of all objections, can be divided into two classes:

A. Objections that are not stated.

B. Objections that are stated.

Objections That Are Not Stated. One of the most difficult situations in selling arises when a prospect has in mind an objection which he considers valid but which he will not express. Possibly he is a bit ashamed of it.

The cure for a situation such as this is obvious: Since you cannot answer objections until you know what they are, your one hope is to smoke out the objection.

How to Smoke Out Objections. Here are some suggestions for getting prospects to state their objections:

1. Give the prospect a chance to talk. Most salesmen talk so much and so fast that they give the prospect little chance to state his objections.

2. Ask questions designed to smoke out objections. These questions may be asked either in the course of the sales talk or near the end of it.

If at the end of your talk, the prospect declines to buy, it often pays to ask him point blank for his reasons. "Something is holding you back, Mr. Prospect. Please tell me the real reason why you are not willing to buy now."

Objections That Are Stated. We come now to the most common form of objection—the objection that the prospect voluntarily states to the salesman.

It is interesting to note that the stating of an objection may result from various mental attitudes of the prospect. The experienced salesman is often able to determine just about what the prospect is thinking when he brings up such an objection. The inexperienced salesman need not feel, however, that he must be a mind reader to handle objections successfully. It is fortunately true that in most cases, if the salesman answers this or any other objection according to rule, he will soon learn the prospect's state of mind and will know how to proceed.

One of the most difficult problems a salesman can face is to answer an objection which arises from *prejudice*. A prejudice, according to Webster, is an opinion that is not based on just grounds. Frequently an opinion does not seem to be based on any grounds.

Liberty Hyde Bailey said, "I once asked a farmer why he didn't blast out a certain rock." His answer was, "It's always been there."

Salesmen frequently meet objections based on prejudices which are no more valid than that one.

How to Handle Prejudiced Prospects

Prospects are full of prejudices—and from these prejudices objections often grow. Such objections as "I never buy stocks that are not listed" or "I hate dictating machines" are often mere opinions based on insufficient or incorrect evidence. Often they are vastly harder to handle than objections based on sound reasoning. Prejudiced prospects would rather keep on believing what they believe than to believe what is true.

H. K. Nixon says in his "Principles of Selling," "You cannot smash a prejudice. You cannot overcome it by sneers or jeers or pitying smiles."

Here are some of the rules for dealing with prejudices:

1. Treat a prejudice with respect. Show the customer that you appreciate his point of view. Make him feel that you are sympathetic.

Remember, a prospect's beliefs are vastly important to him —important out of all relation to their intrinsic importance. Men will rarely fight over facts, but often over beliefs.

2. Do not try to overcome a prejudice by arguments. This merely puts the customer on the defensive.

3. After you have made it clear that you recognize the prejudice, ignore it as much as possible.

4. Suggest, tactfully and indirectly, that the prejudice is inconsistent with something else that the customer believes.

How It Works in Practice

How can we put these suggestions into practice? Well, let's suppose that we are dealing with a prospect who is prejudiced against dictating machines. You might say:

"I know just how you feel about dictating machines—that they are cold and mechanical and that it's hard to talk naturally to them. I used to feel that way myself." (You have shown the prospect that you are sympathetic—that you appreciate his point of view.)

"I suppose people felt that way when they gave up horses in favor of automobiles. They had a real affection for a good horse—the automobile was just machinery. In your lifetime, right in your own store, you have given up the old cash drawers for cash registers; you have installed adding machines—even though you had to let some old clerks go; you have replaced cashboys with pneumatic tubes. So what is more natural than that you carry your efficiency campaign one step further by installing a dictating machine?" (The salesman has here shown that his prejudice against dictating machines is inconsistent with his use of cash registers, adding machines, and pneumatic tubes.)

Sometimes this technique will work, sometimes not. Sometimes nothing will work.

Some prospects just never will be convinced.

Ted Husing was quoted in the New York *Post* as telling of the man on the subway platform who decided to weigh himself at a card machine. He dropped a penny and out came a card: "You weigh 161 pounds. You're doomed to failure." He shrugged, removed his overcoat, and mounted the scales

again. He received the same card: "You weigh 161 pounds.
You're doomed to failure." His anger mounted, and he removed his shoes before weighing himself. But still he received
the same card. Although his train had arrived, the maddened
man then removed all his clothes and, stripped naked, again
mounted the scales and dropped his penny into the slot. Out
came the card: "You still weigh 161 pounds, and you're still
doomed to failure. You didn't think we were fooling, did
you?"

When Should You Answer?

One question that faces the salesman when an objection
is raised is, *"When* shall I answer it?" You can answer it
(*A*) before it is raised, (*B*) when it is raised, (*C*) later, or
(*D*) never.

A. Answering Objections Before They Are Raised. Occasionally it pays to answer an objection before it is asked.

The only excuse for doing this is that you feel reasonably
certain that it will be raised.

For example, the writer once directed the sale of a preferred utility stock. It was being sold considerably above the
prevailing market for similar securities, a fact that was virtually always thrown at the salesman. Therefore, all salesmen
made it a practice to answer this objection before it was
raised. One of them would say, "If this stock sold at $120 a
share, it would be cheap." Then, when he finally broke the
news that the price was $107.50, the prospect was somewhat
prepared for the shock.

It gives a ring of sincerity to your talk—it shows the prospect that you are willing to talk of the bad points as well as
the good points of the security.

If the salesman raises the objection, the prospect does not feel a responsibility for defending it. If the prospect brings it up, he does feel such a responsibility.

Just because the salesman feels it necessary to answer an objection in advance, it does not follow that he must state it in the form of an objection. That is, he does *not* say, "Now, Mr. Jones, of course you are going to say, 'I don't like XYZ Common because it is not listed.'" Instead of stating it as an objection, he turns it around and makes an advantage out of it. He could say, for instance: "One point you will like about XYZ Common, I feel sure, is that it is not listed. You know why some of the largest banks in New York took their stocks off the Big Board."

It should be pointed out, however, that only a few objections must be answered in advance.

B. Answering Objections as Soon as They Are Stated. The best time to answer objections, as a rule, is as soon as they are stated. How they are to be answered will be treated later in this chapter.

C. When the Answering of Objections Should Be Postponed. Under certain circumstances it is advisable to put off answering objections. Instead of taking them up as they are given, you say, "I shall come to that in a minute."

Listed below are some of the circumstances in which it is advisable to postpone the answer to an objection:

If the objection is immaterial, it is often best to postpone the answer, especially if you feel that a prospect is putting up objections just to throw you off your stride.

Maybe He Has No Money—But . . . !

An example of the trivial objection is the one so familiar in many lines: "I have no money." This may be a valid and true objection. Yet if it is raised in the early part of the sales talk, before desire is aroused, it is probably a trivial objection not worth the dignity of a retort.

Another time you should postpone the answer to an objection is when the answer will be long and involved and will interfere with the progress of your sales talk.

A third reason for postponing an answer is that you are not equipped with the facts necessary to make a truthful and convincing answer. In that case the answer has to be postponed until you get the facts. If you must postpone the answer, treat the objection lightly. If you can say so truthfully, make some such statement as, "This, of course, is not important but I shall be glad to get the information for you."

Salesmen should never guess at answers to objections. If you do not know the answer, admit it frankly and state that you will see to it that at some later time, the prospect is supplied with the true and authentic facts. Then be sure that you do supply them.

D. Some Objections Should Never Be Answered. The objection which should not be answered at all is the petty objection. If it is not worth answering, why bother to answer it? Either pass along and forget it or wave it aside as unworthy of notice.

George Biggs of the Vacuum Oil Company told about this experience in *Printers' Ink:*

I was calling with a salesman who had been on the job only a few weeks. After two calls we visited a dealer who had the reputation of being hard to sell. With little introduction this dealer started telling us all about what was wrong with our line. He gave objections 4, 16, and 22 in almost the exact words we have them in the sales manual. He talked nearly five minutes without giving us a chance to get a word in edgewise. I was afraid that the salesman, being pretty green, would not have the answers to these objections in good enough shape to handle them properly. But to my surprise he ignored them. He fished in his pocket for a moment after the dealer had finished his tirade and then brought up a postcard order blank. "Yes," he remarked casually, "I knew that was the way you felt about it. You remember I was here about three weeks ago. I have been thinking over what you said and I believe you could start out with an initial stock about like this and make some money." With that he handed over the postcard on which a suggested order had been drawn up, and the dealer signed it.

Selling Maxims

"Can anybody remember when times were not hard and money not scarce?"—EMERSON.

A lot of salesmen are too busy worrying over objections to give their prospects a chance to buy.

"Jesting often cuts hard knots more effectively than gravity."—HORACE.

Good manners and soft words have answered a lot of objections.

Anybody can be polite over an order, but it takes a gentleman to be courteous in answering an objection.

Nothing is responsible for more false hopes than a polite put-off.

Don't confuse price and value—they're different.

A rebuff should be followed by a rebound.

If you're generous enough to give a customer the company's profit, he'll be generous enough to take it.

People want to keep on believing what they believe—so tie your proposition to their present belief.

If your prospect starts on a controversial subject, smile and change the subject, even if you agree with him.

Never dodge a serious objection—meet it head on.

CHAPTER TWENTY-TWO

Five Ways to Answer Objections

We like a man to come right out and say what he thinks—if we agree with him.

—MARK TWAIN.

At least five standard ways of answering objections are in common use by salesmen:

1. Turn the objection around into a reason for buying. One sales manager has repeatedly issued this challenge: "No matter what the objection is, I can answer it by saying, 'Why, Mr. Blank, that is the very reason you should buy.'"

Every salesman should perfect himself in this particular technique of answering objections. It is not just a showy stunt; it is based on sound common sense.

This policy was taught to National Cash Register salesmen many years ago. When a man states his objection, he reveals his principal reason for not buying. If the salesman can turn that objection into a reason for buying, he will have an excellent chance to get the sale.

It happens again and again that the real reason why the prospect has decided not to buy is actually the very reason why he should buy.

For example, the prospect for an automobile says, "I don't need a new car—I don't drive very much." The salesman can answer: "That's the very reason why you should buy a new

187

188 THE FIVE GREAT RULES OF SELLING

car. You don't drive that old car because you aren't proud of it, because you are afraid it will break down. Now if you buy a new car . . ."

For another example, the prospect for a public-speaking course says, "I don't need a course—I am rarely called on to speak." The salesman replies: "That's the very reason you ought to take the course. You are rarely called on to speak because, as you admit, you do not make a good speech. After you take the course and become a good speaker, you will be called on more often."

This is an effective way to answer objections. We recommend that you try it.

2. Let the prospect answer his own objection. Often the salesman can get the prospect to answer his own objection—or to admit that it is not a valid objection.

Let the objector talk. Perhaps this is all he wants to do anyway. As some philosopher put it, "Many a man would rather you heard his story than granted his request." So let the man who objects talk. Maybe he will answer his own argument. In any event, he will lower his steam pressure and cool off.

The salesman may say, for example: "I am much interested in this point, Mr. Blank. I wish you would explain it to me more fully." Or he may merely ask him, "Why do you believe this?"

If, as so often happens, the objection is not a valid one and the prospect has at best only a half-baked idea of what he is talking about, he will usually flounder around awhile and end by admitting that the matter is of no importance.

"The best way of answering a bad argument," said Sydney Smith, "is to let it go on."

Salesmen should handle this method of answering objections with real sincerity. Never let the prospect suspect that you are giving him a chance to make a display of his ignorance. Say, "What is your opinion about this?" Then listen courteously to his answer.

If the salesman's position is sound and if the objection is not valid, then the salesman, by asking just the right questions, can gradually direct the prospect's explanation to the point where he will end by admitting that his objection is not important and perhaps has no foundation whatever.

A good example of letting the objector answer his own objection was given by W. Hatfield in "I Find Australia." He wrote:

So at the ripe age of nineteen the youth came up from a Midland industrial city to London with a fortnight's board in his pocket and the determination to work his way as a steward. He climbed every gangway in seven miles of docks, but whenever he reached a chief steward he was met with the same question: "Got your discharge book?"—followed by: "What? Never been to sea before? Sorry." He finally countered with the poser: "Had you ever been to sea before, before you'd been to sea?" The chief was so astounded by this retort that he took the retorter on.

3. Explain away the objection. The normal way to answer an objection is, of course, to explain to the prospect the true situation—to show him why he is wrong in thinking what he does.

In other words, give him the facts. Assume that he has not raised an objection but that he has asked a question. For example, when the prospect says, "Your price is too high," just pretend that he asked, "Why is your price higher than that of some of your competitors?" and tell him why it is higher.

One of the best ways to answer an objection is by citing an analogous case.

Suppose, for example, a prospect said to the magazine salesman, "I wouldn't have time to read more magazines." The salesman could answer: "Before you bought your new cabin cruiser you didn't dream that you could find time to spend hours, days, weeks cruising around in it, did you? But, when you began to get so much enjoyment out of it, you just made opportunities, didn't you? It's the same with this magazine. When you find how much information and enjoyment and stimulation it will give you, you will easily find time to read it."

Salesmen are advised to be alert to discover ways of answering objections by citing analogous cases, since they are ordinarily effective.

A variation of this method of meeting objections is by telling an appropriate joke. This is useful when the objection is unimportant or when the prospect is merely trying to put off making a decision.

Thus to a put-off like "Come around April 1 and perhaps I can do something then," you might reply: "That reminds me of the excited would-be passenger who ran up to the information man in the station and said, 'Can I catch the five o'clock express for Jonesville?" The information man answered, 'That depends on how fast you can run. It started three minutes ago.' We can't offer this item after the fifteenth, and therefore, if you are planning to buy . . ."

In answering objections by telling jokes, bear in mind that certain people are practically devoid of a sense of humor, and be guided accordingly.

A still better way to answer an objection is with an example.

Instead of saying, "You're mistaken," you say, "John Jones thought just what you think—let me tell you what he found out."

Let us suppose that you are selling an electric dishwasher and you meet the objection: "I don't believe it will wash off food that has hardened on dishes." You say: "John Jones thought just what you think. So I asked him to save up a couple of dishes that would be hard to clean. They *were* hard to clean—egg on one, mutton tallow on the other. I let Mr. Jones operate the machine himself. He admitted to me after he had finished washing them that the dishes were as clean as the day they were made."

Be on the lookout for interesting examples you can use to answer objections.

4. Admit the objection. Certain objections to buying can not be overcome—for the reason that they are valid, true, and unanswerable.

Nothing is perfect.

A government bond may be nearly 100 per cent safe but the yield is low. Some oil-royalty companies pay enormous so-called "dividends" but they may not be safe. People who buy anything buy it in spite of certain valid objections.

If the objection is valid, the best course is to admit it— and then point out how the objection is outweighed by the other advantages of the article or service you are selling.

For example, if you were selling municipal bonds and the prospect said, "Yes, but the yield is low," it would be idle to attempt to prove that the yield in good municipals is high. Instead you would point out the safety of principal of this security and would try to show that the safety factor outweighs the low yield.

One advantage of admitting an objection is that it impresses the prospect with your sincerity and fairness.

"Lincoln's methods teach us much," says "The Silent Partner." "He would give away six points to carry the seventh, for the whole case depended on the seventh point. He would trade off trivial things to carry the big thought."

Here is an example to prove that you buy things in spite of the fact that there is some objection to them. Sidney Edlund says that he was fired from his first job. He felt that his life was ruined, that nobody would ever give him another job. The next time he was interviewed about a job, naturally he was asked,

"Why did you leave your last job?"

Edlund shuddered. Here was the unanswerable objection to hiring him. He met it head on by admitting it. He said, "I was fired for calling the boss a skunk."

"Was he a skunk?" asked the employer.

"Yes, he was."

"I believe you," said the employer, "and you can start work Monday."

He got the job in spite of the objection.

5. Deny the objection. To answer an objection by denying it is sometimes good practice. Here are some of the circumstances under which it is justified:

If the objection is obviously untrue. Suppose your prospect says, "I have no money," you could say, "Pshaw, I don't believe that," without giving offense.

Another reason for answering an objection by denying it is that the objector does not mean or only half means the objection. For example, when a life insurance salesman came to me the other day I said, quite pleasantly, "Of course this life insurance game is pretty much of a racket." To which he replied: "Of course you don't mean that, Mr. Whiting."

Always enter a denial if the prospect questions your own honesty or integrity or that of your house or any of its officers. In such a case you have no alternative but to enter a firm denial since he cannot answer that sort of an argument with arguments, reasons, or talk. (As Emerson said, "The louder he talked of his honor, the faster we counted our spoons.")

Still, a salesman can enter a denial without losing his dignity or his politeness.

Charles W. Mears, in his book "Salesmanship for the New Era," recommends this course:

Let the salesman take a deep breath or two, look directly at the prospect, and say slowly and clearly—"I don't believe I quite understand what you say." That gives the prospect a chance to cool down and soften what he says, if he sees wisdom in doing so.

If the prospect repeats the obnoxious statement, even then there are better ways of responding than to blurt out, "That's just a plain, malicious lie, and you know it, you human boll weevil."

If the salesman says, "Well, fortunately, for me that doesn't happen to be the real story," or "I have some facts that do not altogether agree with what you say," he makes it clear to his prospect that he is not intimidated and is ready to proceed with his presentation.

Denial is sometimes necessary, even at the loss of a sale. Some salesmen have won respect with their trade by becoming known as men who can't be intimidated, whom nobody can bluff.

Maxims

A tennis player is doomed if he begins hurrying his strokes in a tight match. So is the salesman who lets himself be hurried in the pinches.

"There is hardly anything in the world that some man cannot make a little worse and sell a little cheaper, and the people who consider price only are that man's lawful prey." JOHN RUSKIN.

"To silence another, first be silent yourself."—SENECA.

"There is no good in arguing with the inevitable. The only argument available with an east wind is to put on your overcoat."—JAMES RUSSELL LOWELL.

CHAPTER TWENTY-THREE

Some General Rules for Answering Objections

The best time for the salesman to say nothing is when a prospect wants to say something.

Rule 1: Listen with sincere interest to the objection. In many cases it is wise to repeat the objection in your own words. F. Alexander Magoun of the Massachusetts Institute of Technology said:

I have found in my work that it is a very good technique, when you disagree with another man, to listen to his statement and then to say to him, "Now, as I understand it, your position is so-and-so." And then you proceed to explain his position in your own words and do a better job at it than he can do. Then he knows you understand. Once he knows you understand, he is willing to listen to you. But up to that point, all he is trying to do is hit you over the head.

Then you say, "Well, now, I see that your position is so-and-so. But have you thought of this?" And then you can tell him your story and he will listen to you.

Rule 2: Get into the right mental attitude.

"Selling is not conquest. It is cooperation. Businessmen do not want to be fought. They want to be taught. People would rather buy than be sold."—F. W. Nichol, vice-president and general manager of the International Business Machines Corporation.

Your attitude throughout any sales talk should be an attitude of service. You have called on the prospect to render him a service—to point out to him how he can best supply some want.

Part of your service is to present the facts to him. If the objection he makes is not a valid one, he either does not know the facts or does not correctly interpret them. Your job is not to bring him around to what *you* think; your job is to give him the facts—and let him interpret them for himself.

Naturally you do it gladly, courteously.

"The test of a man's or woman's breeding is how they behave in a quarrel. Anybody can behave well when things are going smoothly."—The Philanderer.

If you will always bear in mind that you are on a mission of service, you will never become disturbed by an objection. If you do, your prospect is likely to think, "Ah, I've caught him now." Immediately the prospect is on the offensive and the salesman on the defensive. Try never to let the prospect put you on the defensive.

Don't think of objections as objections but as questions. Take them as seriously as though they were questions—and no more so. If you act as though they were not important to you, they may not seem too important to the prospect either.

Agree with Him About Something

Rule 3: Find some point of agreement with your prospect.

Although this point is presented near the end of the discussion of objections, it is one of the most important of all rules. Therefore be sure to remember this rule: *No matter what the objection is* (so long as it is valid and reasonable), in answering it *try to find some point of agreement with the prospect.*

Why?

Well, consider the state of mind of the prospect. He believes there is some good reason for not buying. He states that reason. Suppose you answer by saying, "Why, Mr. Blank, that's not so. You are crazy to think a thing like that." What happens? Mr. Blank's feelings are hurt. You are giving no consideration to a pet idea of his. At once he goes to the defense of his objection. And what happens then? You are launched into an argument—a dispute.

Therefore, instead of starting right off to tell the prospect why he is wrong, you should get into step with him, should agree with him about something. For example: "I quite understand how you feel, Mr. Blank. I had the same feeling when this was first presented to me, but. . . ." Or, "I am glad you brought up that point, Mr. Blank." (Look glad! You ought to—your prospect is interested.)

For another example, your prospect may say, "I don't believe in insurance" (or whatever it is you are selling). You can weaken his position by saying, "Neither do I." Then pause before you go on with, "Unless . . ." This "Neither do I, unless . . ." is an effective way to start answering an objection that starts off with "I don't believe."

Note that you have greatly lessened the danger of getting into an argument by agreeing with your prospect—on some immaterial point. His first feeling is that you are going to agree with him all the way through. By the time he finds out that you have merely agreed on some minor point, perhaps you have given him enough facts to swing him around to your point of view.

An example of agreeing with the customer was given by Richard C. Borden in a talk before the Sales Executive Club in New York. He stated that a department store in the West had girls to handle complaints who could, on short notice, become practically hysterical over the phone. When a customer phoned in a complaint, the girl would be horrified that such a mistake could be made—would blame the store, the management, the clerk, herself—would pile it on so thick and so loud that finally the customer would try to calm down the girl by explaining that the fault was not nearly as bad as she was making out. The customer usually ended by admitting that everything was all right.

Such excessive agreement is neither practical nor necessary —nor even quite ethical—for a salesman; but the principle is sound.

Cushion Your Answers

Benjamin Franklin said in his autobiography:

I made it a rule to forbear all direct contradictions to the sentiments of others and all positive assertion of my own. I even forbad myself the use of every word or expression that imported a fixed opinion, such as *certainly, undoubtedly,* etc., and I adopted, instead of them, *I conceive, I apprehend, or I imagine* a thing to be so and so; or it *so appears to me at present.* When another asserted something I thought an error, I denied myself the pleasure of contradicting him abruptly and of showing immediately some absurdity in his proposition; and, in answering, I began by observing that in certain cases and circumstances his opinion would be right, but in the present case there *appeared* or *seemed* to me some difference, etc. I soon found the advantage of this change in my manner; the conversations I engaged in went on more pleasantly.

John Alford Stevenson says in his book, "Constructive Salesmanship—Principles and Practice": "You will find it a good plan to memorize a number of opening phrases for meeting objections which will serve to make your replies less blunt."

Any successful salesman will recognize the correctness of this practice of getting into step with the prospect and will use it regularly in answering objections.

Act as if It Were a Real Objection

Rule 4: Never treat a prospect's objection contemptuously.

No matter how silly or trivial an objection is, never treat it with contempt. Even though you can answer the objection with a few words, it is usually wiser (if you do not ignore it entirely) to waste a few words to soften your answer.

For example, the prospect for some common stock might say, of a fully paid and nonassessable stock, "I'm afraid they might slap an assessment on my stock." It would be truthful and a complete answer to say, "The stock is non-assessable," but it would not be courteous. It is safer and better to soften your answer by saying, "That is a good point. A stock that is subject to assessment is a dangerous thing. It well repays anyone to check this point with every stock he buys. It happens in this case, however, Mr. Blank, that the articles of incorporation of this company provide that the stock cannot be assessed under any circumstances. So you are perfectly safe."

Yes, but suppose your prospect treats your sales talk contemptuously?

Albert S. Osborn, a neighbor of mine and one of the leading handwriting experts of the world, tells a story of a salesman who came to his office years ago and sold him $2 worth of mucilage that wouldn't stick. Mr. Osborn refers to the incident as "the time I got stuck with the mucilage." After the salesman left and Mr. Osborn realized that he had been "stuck," he developed a three-rule technique for turning down salesman that is worth thinking about. Here it is: Rule 1:— Ask the price and insist on getting it. Rule 2:—Put in a strong negative. "No, I don't want it and won't have it." Rule 3:— Treat the situation with levity (or, to put it in salesmen's slang, "Kid him out of it").

I should hate to have this technique get noised around among prospects—they're difficult enough now! I never met it in the field, but if I should I think I would say, "I know the idea of buying thus-and-so may seem funny to you— but losing so many dollars a week by not having it isn't so funny."

Don't Waste Too Much Time on Objections

Rule 5: Answer briefly.

Don't treat your prospect's objection contemptuously, but on the other hand, do not treat it too seriously. Use as few words as are practicable. Don't spin out your answers. Don't feel that you have to bury objections in graves ten feet deep. Finish the job promptly and get back into your sales talk. People don't buy because you have answered objections but because they want what you are selling. Get back as quickly as you can to talking about the prospect and his wants and how your goods will supply these wants.

Rule 6: Don't wrangle.

The prospect states his objection. You answer it. If the prospect then shows signs of entering into a lengthy disputation, it is generally best to say something to this effect: "I thoroughly understand your point, Mr. Blank, and I appreciate your explaining to me your feelings on the matter. This, of course, is not an essential point." Then rapidly pick up the thread of your sales talk and move along.

If the prospect is by nature a man who wants to argue and dispute, the one best way to weaken his position and to improve yours is to agree with him and go on with something else.

Rule 7: Never appear to doubt that you have answered the objection completely.

After some salesmen have answered an objection at great length, they have the bad habit of saying, "Now, Mr. Blank, have I made this point clear—do you agree with me that the machine is all right in this respect?"

Why is this a bad practice?

First, because you are asking your prospect to admit that he was wrong—which is an idiotic thing to do. Let your prospect save face.

Moreover, you don't want to give your prospect a chance to spin out the discussion of that point or to raise another objection.

You Have to Stay Awake

Rule 8: Be alert and resourceful.

A book twice as long as "Gone with the Wind" could not give you directions that would cover every objection that could be raised and every problem that could be faced.

Therefore you must depend on yourself. An excellent example of resourcefulness was given by Robert A. Bruce in *Sales Scrap Book Magazine*. In substance his story was that once he called on a buyer for a sugar plantation on Oahu, one of the Hawaiian Islands. This buyer had a reputation for all-round perverseness. As soon as Mr. Bruce got inside this man's office, the buyer began to rave because, he said, salesmen took so much time he could not work. Finally he snarled, "What do you want?" Mr. Bruce replied: "I understand that you once made your living by selling. When you ran across a tough old buzzard like yourself, did you immediately leave the office?" The buyer replied, "No, I stayed with him until I got the order." Whereupon Mr. Bruce sat down and stayed until *he* got the order.

Another good example comes from Alaska, where a certain salmon cannery faced drastic loss because its season's pack consisted almost entirely of white salmon. For decades salmon advertising and pricing had put a premium on red salmon, although that kind is no better. The canner ordered new labels reading, "Genuine Alaskan White (Natural) Salmon—Guaranteed Not to Turn Red in the Can." He received the top market price.

Rule 9: Find the key objection.

Sometimes a prospect will fire a whole broadside of objections at you: "Your price is too high, your styles are behind the times, your deliveries are slow, your credit department is dictatorial."

When this happens, answer only the important objection—and get back to your selling.

Rule 10: When you have answered an objection, do not pause. Jump right back into your sales talk.

The reason you should go quickly back into your presentation is to keep the prospect from piling one objection on top of another and thus breaking up the continuity of your talk.

So as soon as you have answered an objection, get right back into your sales talk.

From the foregoing discussion of objections and how to answer them, the salesman will see that as long as he knows the rules, it is a relatively simple matter to answer objections —even to use the answers as stepping stones in reaching up for the order.

Selling Maxims

Reasoning against a prejudice is like fighting against a shadow; it exhausts the reasoner, without visibly affecting the prejudice.

"A dispute is continued by the desire of conquest, till vanity kindles into rage, and opposition rankles into enmity."— SAMUEL JOHNSON.

The hotter the argument, the colder the prospect.

Prejudice was not reasoned into your prospects and cannot be reasoned out.

CHAPTER TWENTY-FOUR

How to Get In

If an important man were to take time to see everybody who wanted to see him, he wouldn't be important long.
—ANONYMOUS.

If you expect to find, in this chapter or anywhere else, an unfailing rule for getting you in to see the man you want to see at the time you want to see him, you should harden yourself for disappointment.

No universal door opener exists.

If important executives saw everyone who wanted to see them, they would have time for little else. So they are forced to protect themselves with receptionists and secretaries.

The best general rule is to be prepared to prove to the prospect or his guards that you are in a position to render your prospect a real service. If you are, you are entitled to get in; if you aren't, you don't deserve to get in.

Here are some further rules for getting past receptionists and secretaries.

Rules for Getting In

Rule 1: You must feel, dress, talk, and act the part of a man who expects to get in.

You must feel that you have a *right* to be ushered in.

You get this feeling by knowing so much about your prod-

204

uct and what it will do, so much about your prospect and what he needs done, that you would feel sorry for your prospect if you did not get in to see him.

For example, when I was in charge of sales promotion for Dale Carnegie Institute and an unknown printing salesman called, I always referred him to Dick Fay, our purchasing agent. But when Fred Peck of George Bosch and Company called, I always saw him. Fred knew so much about printing and had made such a study of our problem of getting students that his sales talks were worth listening to. He had helped us distribute our printed matter at meetings, had kept a line on the results of our mailing campaigns, and knew what we were trying to do.

Fred Peck always got in because he had earned the right to get in.

Good Clothes Help

You must *dress* the part.

For example, a man who used to sell magazine subscriptions on Wall Street wore a cutaway coat, striped trousers, a plug hat, and a carnation; and he carried a cane. He looked as though he had just stepped out of a society wedding. When he announced, "I have come to see Mr. J. P. Morgan," he managed to make it sound as though he were conferring a favor on Mr. Morgan. He told me he was rarely refused admittance.

I don't recommend cut-aways and plug hats for ordinary salesmen, but I do recommend that they dress like successful businessmen.

If you dress like a tramp you will be treated like a tramp.

You must *talk* the part. Don't talk like a beggar or a pencil

peddler. "Will you please tell Mr. Blank that . . ." tells
the story better than "I'd like to see Mr. Blank." The former
makes for action, the latter invites questions.

You must *act* the part. Remember, if you *act* as though
you expected to get in you will *feel* as though you expected
to get in. How do you *act* the part?

1. Walk in briskly.

2. If you have to wait, don't slouch down in your chair as
though you had come for a week end.

3. Make it a general rule not to wait longer than fifteen
minutes for anyone. (Naturally, you have to make exceptions.) Keep looking at your watch and consulting your note-
book as you wait. At the end of fifteen minutes say to the
receptionist, "I must leave in a moment for another appointment." Often she will try then to get you in. If not, ask her
to phone the secretary of the man you are calling on for a
definite appointment. Say, "Will you please see if Mr. Blank
can see me at 3:15 on Thursday?"

Get Your Customer to Get You In

Rule 2: Use the "radiation," or "endless chain," method.

That is, you get a customer to give you names of prospects.
Then, with his permission, use his name or some form of
introduction by him (a card, or letter, or a phone call of
introduction) to get you past the guardians of the gate.

Rule 3: Use letters to get in. How? Here are some suggestions:

Send the prospect a letter signed by the head of the company. In selling for the Dale Carnegie Institute, we found
that a letter signed by Dale Carnegie practically always as-

sured us admittance. When a newspaper organization was selling its preferred stock it made effective use of a letter to prospects signed by the head of the company—a nationally known figure.

Send the prospect an "I'll call unless" letter. B. W. Brown used to send important men a letter that said in substance: "I would like to talk with you briefly about a matter I am sure is of importance to you. Unless I hear to the contrary, I shall call at 3:45 on Wednesday." He found that a certain number of men would neglect to head him off. He felt he was justified in calling on these men and saying to their secretaries, "I have an appointment at 3:45 with Mr. Blank." This is slightly "high-pressure"—but it works.

Try writing letters in longhand. Almost anybody, no matter how important, will read a letter written in longhand, especially if it is on good stationery.

An oil-royalty salesman told me, "If I write five longhand letters a night I can get enough prospects to keep going."

Use well-written form letters. Be sure to call within two or three days after the letters are received by the prospects.

A novel formula for following up a company mailing is used by Arthur J. Hand of New York, as told in *Sales Scrap Book:*

I call the day after the literature is received. If I am not aware of the name of the proper person to be interviewed, I use the following dialogue:

SALESMAN: May I speak to the credit manager? For the moment I forget his name.

BUFFER. Oh, yes! Mr. Smith.

SALESMAN: (*hands card to buffer*). Will you kindly tell Mr. Smith that Mr. Hand is here.

BUFFER: Mr. Smith wants to know what it's all about.

SALESMAN: My company sent him a letter and he did not answer. The prospect ordinarily does not wish to be criticized for not answering mail and hence tells the buffer to let the salesman in.

Cards Help—Sometimes

Rule 4: If you use cards, use them as they should be used.

The best general rule for using ordinary business cards to get in is: Don't.

As a rule, the man who peddles many cards makes few sales.

The exceptions:

(*a*) When your company is big and important (which does not apply in the case of insurance companies).

(*b*) When there is nothing on your card but your name. Some salesmen fold over a corner of the card—enough to cover the name. This arouses curiosity.

After your call is over, it sometimes pays to leave your card—though generally it goes into the wastebasket.

One of the best ways to use a card is to have a blank one and to write on it a message which arouses the prospect's curiosity or which tells him briefly how he will benefit by using your product.

For example, in selling a sales course we would send a card to the president of the company. It read, "In 10 minutes I can tell you how to increase sales 10 per cent." It worked.

Rule 5: Get in with a gift. What if Fuller did make it famous! Insurance men have used this gift plan with good results.

Realsilk used a gadget—a free mending kit for silk stockings. The salesman would get into the house to explain its use.

The salesmen of the California Fruit Growers' Exchange, sellers of Sunkist oranges, lemons, and grapefruit, used to get in with a gadget by which the store owner could automatically calculate the number of dozens of lemons or oranges per box, the cost to him per dozen, and the price he had to charge the consumer to provide him with a gross profit of twenty-five per cent.

The Minneapolis-Honeywell Regulator Company provided its salesmen with two gadgets that were useful in getting interviews with architects. One was a fuel-saving guide and the other a device for figuring heat losses as a result of wind.

Walter Lowen of New York, who has secured jobs for nearly 50,000 people, tells this story of a unique way of getting in:

A young man wanted a job with an advertising company that specialized in novelty in its copy writing. This ingenious young man got a homing pigeon, put it in a cage, took it to the manager's office, and when he was out to lunch succeeded in having it put on his desk. He had written a letter to go with the pigeon. The letter outlined his qualifications for the job and asked the manager to attach his answer to the pigeon's leg and set it free. That afternoon the pigeon returned to the sender. The note on the leg band said Yes. The next day the applicant went in for a personal interview and got the job.

Lowen's comment is, "A stunt alone won't put you over, but sometimes it will open the door for you."

"I Want Only Three Minutes" May Turn the Trick

Rule 6: Make the request seem small.

Many men fear salesmen because salesmen waste time.

A salesman I know who sold a service used to place a stop watch ostentatiously on his prospect's desk and say, "In exactly ten minutes you'll say you're interested or I'll say good-by."

Dick Sanborn, a veteran New York salesman, was a great believer in asking for "three minutes."

When a receptionist asked him his business, he would say: "Do you mind saying I'm here? Then, if he does not see me, all right. Just tell him I'm here."

"Does he know you?"

"He doesn't know me but I hope he will soon."

"What do you want to see him about?"

"If he'll allow me to speak to him for three minutes, he'll know whether or not he wants to talk with me. I'll leave at the end of three minutes unless he asks me to stay."

If Dick ever walked into the presence of a prospect who then did not want to talk with him, he would smile and say, "You look like a good-natured person. You have to earn a living. So do I. I want to earn mine by talking to you for three minutes—how about it?"

Be Friends with Everybody

Rule 7: Try to make friends with everybody in the office. Salesmen who have been turned down by secretaries have often been smuggled in by an office boy.

My friend the late Walter Jenkins was always able to walk in on one of the most important space buyers in New York. I asked him once how it happened.

He said; "I helped to raise that boy. When I started in as an advertising solicitor, he had just started in as an office boy.

I liked him, was nice to him, and made a fuss over him. He
has never forgotten it and is never likely to."

Rule 8: Get your prospect to do you a favor. Many a prospect who will turn down a salesman will grant a favor—
especially if he gains a feeling of importance by doing so.

The idea is not new. Ben Franklin wrote in his autobiography:

> My first promotion was my being chosen, in 1736, clerk of the
> General Assembly. The choice was made that year without opposi-
> tion; but the year following, when I was again proposed, a new
> member made a long speech against me, in order to favor some other
> candidate.
>
> I did not like the opposition of this new member. I did not, how-
> ever, aim at gaining his favor by paying any servile respect to him,
> but, after some time, took this other method. Having heard that he
> had in his library a certain very scarce and curious book, I wrote
> a note to him, requesting he would do me the favor of lending it to
> me for a few days. He sent it immediately. When we next met in
> the House, he spoke to me (which he had never done before); and
> he ever manifested a readiness to serve me on all occasions, so that
> we became great friends. This is another instance of the truth of
> an old maxim I had learned, which says, "He that has once done
> you a kindness will be more ready to do you another, than he whom
> you yourself have obliged."

Rule 9: Offer service. If you can truthfully send in word
to your prospect that you can show him how to increase production, cut costs, save on his income tax, or cut ten strokes
off his score, he is likely to see you. The more specific it is
and the more truthful it sounds, the more likely you are to
get in.

He May Not Be Too Busy Tomorrow

Rule 10: Ask for an appointment. Many men who will send word that they are too busy to see you today will weaken and give you an appointment for some future time—if you ask for it.

"We recently heard of a successful New York salesman," says *Managers Magazine*, "who, though his clients were big businessmen with tough schedules and many important appointments, rarely had difficulty in getting an appointment whenever he asked for one. This astounding record he explained by the fact that he always asked for an appointment at an odd time. That is, instead of suggesting eleven o'clock, for instance, he would specify 10:50. Of course the busy executive would have another engagement at eleven, but few would have thought of asking to see him at the odd hour. The executive also somehow got the idea that this salesman's time was valuable and that he would be interested in making the interview as concise as possible."

Rule 11. Use some ingenuity. There is always a way to get in—if you will only take the trouble to find it.

A story in *Gas Age Record* tells of the ingenious strategy of one Morton M. Chorost, sales manager for the State Appliance Company, Newark.

He called on a barber; the barber was busy and said, "Go 'way, mister, I no gotta time to talk salesman. Customer come in, I give him the haircut. Good bye, please!"

Morton M. Chorost didn't hesitate. He flipped his hat onto a hook, doffed his coat and seated himself in the barber's chair.

"Give me a shave, John," he said.

But that was one time when the barber didn't do the talking.

He listened to Chorost. It took a total of four shaves in as many days for Morton to get his story across, but when he got out of the chair for the last time, the barber had signed an order for a gas-fired unit heater installation.

Don't Talk—on the Doorstep!

How about when you are "half in"? Suppose your prospect comes into the hall and asks you to state your business—what should you do?

The rule is: Don't hit him! The provocation is great but the results are bad.

Try some of these remarks:

"Let's step back into your office, where we can talk without interruption"—and start walking. Unless he is an utter boor, he will follow—but he probably is or he would not insist on talking in the hall.

"I don't think you'd want your employees (or 'outsiders,' if there are no employees in sight) to hear what I have to say —may I go back to your office?"

"I'm sorry you are too busy to see me now. May I see you Thursday at 9:40?"

Meet it head on. What is the rule if the prospect still insists on hearing your story in the hall?

The rule is: Don't tell it.

I can *imagine* exceptions but I never saw one. You lose your self-respect when you talk in "No-man's land." And you don't make the sale.

CHAPTER TWENTY-FIVE

How to Get In When It's Difficult

A salesman's Purgatory is fear of guarded doors.
—ANONYMOUS.

"All right," you say, "but suppose you have tried all the tricks and you find you face a secretary who insists on knowing your mission, and so you finally break down and admit that you sell insurance or bonds or mucilage, and the secretary says, 'He doesn't want any—good-by.'—then what?"

Then you're in what Georgians call a "tight."

How do you wriggle out? Sometimes you don't. Your best chance is to sell the secretary. Sort of a semifinal bout!

The secretary will often be harder to sell than the boss. Don't be too casual about it. Give the secretary just as good a sales talk as you would give the boss. Once you have her believing that the boss ought to know about it, you're in.

For years I had a secretary, Miss Mary Ann McGaffin, who was brutal to salesmen. Once in a great while she would come into the office and say shamefacedly, "There's a salesman outside I think you ought to see." I'd see him—if for no other reason than to have a look at the man who had sold Miss Mac.

What Not to Do

Here are some don'ts for those who want to know how to get in.

Don't No. 1: *Don't lie.* Your business is not "personal," not "confidential," and probably not too "important" to anyone but you.

Don't No. 2: *Don't use a trick.* A. H. Deute told in *Printers' Ink* of a salesman who got past his secretary by telling her he had heard that Mr. Deute was an excellent judge of sales talks and he wanted a few minutes of personal criticism. It turned out that the man was a book agent and that he regularly used that ruse to get in.

Don't No. 3: *Don't be afraid to tell secretaries what your business is.* They usually have a right to know. Don't fence with them and antagonize them. Tell them and try to enlist their help. As Margaret Brown said in *Printers' Ink:* "We [secretaries] would be the best friends salesmen ever had if they'd give us the chance." Do you think for a minute a woman who has a responsible position is proof against a sales suggestion like: "Miss Brown, if I could show you how to save a thousand dollars a year in office expense, would you give me ten minutes of your time?" or "Miss Brown, I've got a market study here that Mr. President would find valuable. Now should I go into the details with you—or whom would you suggest I talk to?"

No supersecretary, assistant, buffer, or whatever name you have for these hard-to-get-past women is going to run the risk of preventing her chief and her firm from getting really worthwhile knowledge of a product or service.

Salesmen would get further if they would cultivate the woman whose job it is to conserve, as far as possible, her superior's time. Use her as your sales weapon! Give her all the facts, and all the attention, you would be willing to devote to her chief. And nine times out of ten she'll do your selling for you.

If your sales story is worth telling, don't keep it a secret. Tell it to everyone who will listen.

CHAPTER TWENTY-SIX

Make More Calls

Difficulty is, for the most part, the daughter of idleness.
                                               —JOHNSON.

You say you want to make more sales!

Anyone can tell you how: Make more calls.

Stop and think about it. Don't say, "He can't mean *me*." I *do* mean you.

Are you making as many calls as you can?

No, and you never did—not for any sustained period.

In more than nineteen years as a sales manager, I never saw one single salesman who worked as hard as he could for more than a couple of days at a time—or any sales manager either, including myself.

Most salesmen could make twice as many calls as they do, if they were willing to punish themselves a little.

I was chatting one day in Waco, Texas, with a man who represented a firm of public-relations counselors in Chicago. He said, "I'm tired."

"Why?" I asked.

"I usually make five calls a day," was his answer, "and I usually spend six days in Waco. On account of a convention I can get a room here for only three days. So I've been making ten calls a day."

This man seemed tired, but not exhausted. Yet, if his boss

217

had said, "Why not do it every day?" he would probably have fallen in a swoon!

In all my years as a sales manager, I never knew a salesman to work himself to death—though a lot claimed that they were close to doing that.

Of course, there was the Rockland schoolteacher. He came to work for our security-selling force in Maine back in 1920. He was seventy-two years old—I hired him largely out of charity. He proved to be a natural, a man who couldn't do a selling wrong. But he made the mistake of trying to make up in fifty-two weeks for the fifty-two years he had wasted teaching school and he died trying.

Unless you too are seventy-two years old—or older—never fear that you cannot make more calls without overtaxing your strength. If you have brains enough to add 2 and 2 and make the answer come out 4 with reasonable regularity, then there is no use lecturing you on the law of averages or explaining that (assuming you are now making some sales) if you make more calls you must inevitably make more sales.

Why Salesmen Fail—They Loaf

An inquiry made as to the good qualities of 400 of the most successful salesmen of twenty large insurance companies showed that "willingness to do a full day's work" stood second in the list of qualities.

Of 624 salesmen who were discharged by members of the Chicago Sales Executive Club, nearly a third were parted from the pay roll for lack of industry. In other words, they did not make the calls.

"See the People"

Isn't that at least negative evidence of the contention that you can be more successful if you make more calls?

Here's another example, culled from a Westraco publication:

"You gotta see a lotta people and you gotta see 'em often." That was Eddie Wilson's homespun way of saying that the surest way to get contracts is to make contacts.

Eddie grew up in the heart of the Berkshires. He walked right out of the tenth grade one day into an electric shop as an all-round helper. He couldn't take a sentence apart but he could take a washing machine apart. He couldn't translate Latin but he could transfer heating elements.

It soon developed that he could sell, that he liked to sell, that he had to sell. Before he was twenty-two he was in Rutland working for a major utility company. Once there, he made Vermont sales history on the whole appliance line.

Up at Montpelier you'll still hear the story about Eddie's appearance at a sales convention. He was to give a talk on "How I Tripled My Quota." He had never talked to a group. He became a country boy again, scared stiff. In midafternoon he decided to resort to bottled courage. He reached the depths of the bottle, the heights of assurance, but he had forgotten that cocktails were to be served before dinner! Through the meal he sat dazed, befuddled, bewildered. He was glowingly introduced. He stumbled to his feet, rubbed his hands unsteadily over his face, peered out into a dim sea of faces—murmured: "See the people, see the people, see the people." That was all he said—and yet it was all he had to say to tell his story of sales success.

How to Make More Calls

To make more calls:
1. You must *want to*.
2. You must *plan*.
3. You must *work*.

STEP ONE: *How do you make yourself* want *to make more calls? Sell the idea to yourself—make a sales talk to yourself.*

Don't think your job of selling yourself is completed with one application. You may have to resell yourself about twice a day until you have made it a *habit* to make enough calls. After that, your subconscious mind looks after it.

Don't think you can skip this step of selling yourself and yet succeed in forcing yourself to make more calls. Here is a good way to sell yourself: Sit down and figure the value of your time—how much you earned last year per hour worked. Then consider how much you will make if you work more hours.

When you have done this, set a goal—not of how many calls you are determined to make but how much money you are determined to earn. Then figure out how many calls you have to make to reach that goal.

Don't set your mark too high or you may be like the man Benjamin Franklin tells about in his autobiography, who, having bought an ax from a smith, desired to have the whole of its surface as bright as the edge.

The smith consented to grind it bright for him if he would turn the wheel; he turned, while the smith pressed the broad face of the ax hard and heavily on the stone, which made the turning of it very fatiguing. The man came every now and then from the wheel to see how the work went on, and at length said he would take his ax as it was, without further grinding. "No," said the smith, "turn on, turn on; we shall have it bright by-and-by; as yet, it is only speckled." "Yes," said the man, "but I think I like a speckled ax best."

Once you have done the job of selling yourself on the benefit to you of making more calls, then go on to the next job— the job of organizing your day's work.

You Have to Work Your Brain, Too

STEP TWO FOR MAKING MORE CALLS: *Plan.*

First analyze your time and set up a general plan.

You begin with twenty-four hours in a day! "Astounding," you remark. I know. Yet more human waste and human want and human suffering are due to a failure to recognize that fact than to almost any other failing.

You admit that you have only one thing that's really yours —*time;* that you have twenty-four hours of time in a day and no more; and that if you waste it, it is gone forever. Now let's do something about it.

What would you like to do each working day? Well, here are some of your day's jobs:

Sleeping	Calling
Eating	Missionary calls
Amusement	Call backs
Planning	Just plain calls
Prospecting	Office work
Traveling	Making reports
Waiting	Studying

"So much to do, so little time!"

All right, do your own apportioning. No need to tell you how—just face facts and write figures.

Once you have looked right in the teeth of the appalling fact that you haven't time to half-do half the things you want to do, you come right up to the next step—you must economize time and speed up your activities to get it all done.

Here are some suggestions:

Speed-up Rule No. 1: Study ways to speed up the doing of immaterial things—like shaving, dressing, report making, and the like. How? It's a long story and it will be found in several books on personal efficiency.

Hurry! But Not Too Much

Speed-up Rule No. 2: Determine not to hurt your efficiency. Don't rush your meals. Don't speed up immediately after meals. Don't cut too deeply into your sleeping time. Don't rob yourself entirely of all amusement, but don't overdo it either.

Speed-up Rule No. 3: Don't skimp on your planning time and on your study time.

Now you are ready to work out a tentative daily schedule, with time allotted to all the things you ought to do.

First consider how to make your daily schedule. When should you make your plan for the day's work?

The possibilities are

(*a*) Just before dinner at night, or

(*b*) Just before going to bed. (A poor time, because you are probably too sleepy to plan clearly.)

(*c*) First thing in the morning. This is the best. It requires that you get up early enough to have time for the job, but it rewards you with a clear mind and usually freedom from distractions.

Do not, as a rule, wait to do your planning until you reach the office. It encourages you to sit around when you should be out calling.

All right, it's 7 A.M. and you are ready to plan a day's work.

How to Plan a Day's Work

Here are the steps you must take:

A. Determine your objective. Just what are you going to try to do today?

B. Select the prospects you are going to call on.

C. Route your calls to cut down distance. The less distance you travel, the more calls you can make. A Carnegie Institute of Technology survey showed that 45 per cent of a salesman's working time was taken up by walking and waiting. So note these points:

1. If practicable, make your hardest call first.

2. Have some elasticity to your schedule. Determine what you will do if a prospect is busy or away. Don't go miles to call on one prospect and find yourself with no other prospects in the vicinity.

Speed-up Rule No. 4: Start early. It is amazing how many prospects are astir at 5 A.M. if you only can locate them.

Especially, don't hang around the office or the hotel room. Pretend the chair has a nail in it and that the floor is hot as a stove—and get out! Don't wait for the mail. If anything comes for you, it will keep.

Speed-up Rule No. 5: Speed up your walking.

Speed-up Rule No. 6: Don't talk too long. Especially cut down all conversations except those about business. "Any businessman worth his salt," says *Printers' Ink,* "nowadays has but one real hobby. It's no sport-page hobby. It's a first-page hobby. It's business. Talk that."

Speed-up Rule No. 7: Keep calling.

Speed-up Rule No. 8: Make your lunch brief and light.

Speed-up Rule No. 9: Keep calling.

Speed-up Rule No. 10: Don't stop too early. The average salesman could get in from one to five more calls if he would just keep going.

Speed-up Rule No. 11: Make night calls, if your business permits—and it probably does.

You know all those rules anyway. Of course you do! But can you say that you live up to them?

Some General Rules for Making More Calls

Here are a few more general rules—and you know these too:

1. Keep personal matters out of business hours. No need to enlarge on this. The smart salesmen observe this rule; the dull ones are always looking for a job.

2. Cure yourself of fear. Why? Because many salesmen refrain from making calls not because they are lazy but because they are afraid of being turned down, of competition, of objection, of irascible buyers, of important men. (If you are timid, if you lack poise and self-confidence, take a practical course in public speaking.)

3. Call on men who can decide. Hundreds of thousands of calls are wasted each year in calls on men who do not decide and who finally pass the salesman along—or more probably forget him.

4. Try in every way to cut down your waiting time. Try to get appointments. Call on prospects at the time they are least likely to be busy. Let the receptionist know, politely and tactfully but no less certainly, that you are a busy man and want to cut down waiting time.

STEP THREE FOR MAKING MORE CALLS: *Force yourself to do it.*

"All right," you say, "admitting that I want to make more money and admitting that I'd like to observe the rules, how can I force myself to do it?"

I don't know. The unsolved problem of all time is that of making people do what they ought to do. This point is well made in this little parable from *The Washington Review:*

> With eagerness the young agent asked his manager how he could attain success.
>
> "I'll tell you," the manager said, "how to obtain success by the use of two simple rules.
>
> "The first is: Don't do the things you know you ought not to do."
>
> The young man's face fell.
>
> He had not expected a rule so hard to follow.
>
> "The second is: Do all the things that you know you ought to do."
>
> The young man turned away sadly.
>
> He wanted to succeed without the personal discipline necessary for success.

You will find some suggestions in Chapter 27 for forcing yourself, by drill, to do the things you ought to do. Here are two more rules that will work if you will:

1. In general, the way to make more calls is to make more calls.

You must be your own top sergeant—your own Simon Legree.

Don't worry about it. Don't put it off. Just do it.

Henry Ward Beecher once was asked how he managed to get through so much work in a day. He replied: "By never doing anything twice. I never anticipate my work and never worry about it. When the time comes to do a thing I do it, and that's the end of it."

Stop Believing What You Know Isn't So!

2. Stop believing in fairy tales, in salesmen's saws, in miracles, in voodoos. Stop rationalizing, stop excusing yourself, stop salving your conscience with reasons so feeble a child would blush to use them. For example: Stop believing that:

You will break your health if you work too hard.

You will become so tired you can't make effective calls. It can happen—but it isn't likely to.

You need long week ends, long vacations; that you need to space out one-day holidays into three days.

That rainy days are bad days to call. A few months before this was written, a salesman told me, in all seriousness, that people didn't like to have him call when he was dripping. (He must call on softer-hearted prospects than the average. I never knew a prospect to object because a salesman was uncomfortable. Nor did I ever see one who minded a little rain water on the floor.) Get rainproof. Buy a raincoat and rubbers. Get some snowshoes!

Stop believing that the early days of the week are the best for calling. The Babson Institute made a survey of the calling activities of 755 salesmen and found that these men made 75 per cent more calls on the first three business days of the week than they did on the last three.

Fairy tales! Myths! Rationalizations!

Stop excusing yourself. Don't weaken.

More Calls Will Do It

Make more calls. Work harder.

Does an increased number of calls produce an increase in volume? In 1932, reports *Printers' Ink,* the American Enameled Brick Corporation found itself faced with a shutdown. General Manager Frank Geraghty said to his salesmen,

"Besides doing your regular work, each of you will make ten extra working calls every working day on architects and contractors." The men made more calls. And 10 per cent of these extra calls resulted in so many sales that the factory, instead of shutting down, went into day-and-night production.

Make more calls. This one act may solve all your pressing problems.

When I was a small boy living on a farm in Connecticut, I read in a mail-order paper an advertisement that said: "How to get rich. Send 10¢." It looked like a good buy, so I sent the dime. I got back a piece of rough newsprint paper on which was crudely printed this stirring message: "Work like blazes."

I'm inclined to think that this is Rule 1 of successful selling.

Selling Maxims

When a man says he is going to do this or that tomorrow, ask him what he did yesterday.

A fool can stay up all night, but it takes a man to get up in the morning.

Making a lot of calls will do almost anything for a salesman that supersalesmanship can do—and very many things that it can't.

Spare the shoe leather and spoil the pay check.

"The dog that trots about finds a bone."—Gypsy saying.

"It is not the part of a man to fear sweat."—SENECA.

Expect to make sales, but don't expect them to make themselves.

Most salesmen would be willing to get rich by hard work if it didn't take so much effort.

"Diligence is the mother of sales."—CERVANTES (1947 model).

"God gives every bird his food, but he does not throw it into the nest."—HOLLAND.

CHAPTER TWENTY-SEVEN

How to Become Enthusiastic

Men are failures not because they are stupid, but because they are not sufficiently impassioned.
—STRUTHERS BURT.

The history of selling is crowded with examples of men who sold for one primary reason—that they were enthusiastic.

Dale Carnegie tells in his column of the experience of Harry Wright, who was buried for three years behind the wires of a cashier's cage in an insurance broker's office.

Wright asked for a better job and was refused. He hated the work, he wanted to quit—but even more he wanted to eat.

So he stayed in the cage until his vacation time came. Then he did not go on a pleasure trip, but instead went out and tried to sell life insurance. He was only twenty-two years old at the time. He knew virtually nothing about life insurance. Yet he sold three out of the first five men he called on—on enthusiasm alone.

He never went behind the wires again. He continued to sell—largely on enthusiasm. For sixteen years he sold over a million dollars' worth of insurance a year—still largely on enthusiasm.

If others have through enthusiasm performed miracles of selling, would it not pay you to consider developing a little more of your own?

229

Enthusiasm can be developed by anyone who is willing to follow a few simple rules—and to practice. You develop enthusiasm as you develop your muscle: by exercising it.

A salesman who is naturally unenthusiastic has this choice: to become enthusiastic or to go back to the farm. It doesn't take a lot of enthusiasm to follow a plow.

How can you become enthusiastic? It's quite simple.

1. Learn the rules.

2. Drill yourself.

How to Go about It

Rule 1: Learn more about your product if you wish to become more enthusiastic about it.

Consider the bearing of these two axioms on your problem:

(*a*) If you don't know about it, you don't like it.

(*b*) The more you know about a good product, the more enthusiastic you become about it.

My friend Randy Howland, who used to run an employment agency, gave me this example:

His organization was asked by a big linoleum company to get a salesman for a difficult territory. Mr. Howland secured for this job a man who had been selling linoleum for another company— with only mediocre success.

The reason this man had not been selling, Mr. Howland told the company's sales manager, was that the salesman knew so little about linoleum that he had no enthusiasm for it.

The linoleum company did not send this man on the road at once, but instead kept him in the plant for three months. He actually worked at various jobs in the factory. He helped to *make* linoleum. He saw cork being prepared for various uses. He got the feel of cork, the smell of cork, the taste of cork—got interested in how linoleum was made and how it was used.

As a result of knowing so much about linoleum, he became thoroughly enthusiastic over it.

When he started selling for the new company he was successful almost at once. He was soon made sales manager of one of the company's important Western territories. At last report he was still there, still successful, and still enthusiastic.

He became enthusiastic by learning more about his product—and so can you.

You Will Not Believe This!

Rule 2: If you feel yourself losing your enthusiasm, then work harder, make more calls!

"This just *can't* be right," you say. "Why, it upsets beliefs as old and respectable as the belief that nobody buys on Saturday morning, just before Christmas, or in August."

What does the average salesman do when he is turned down a couple of times and when he feels about as enthusiastic as wilted lettuce?

He quits and goes to the pictures. I've heard sales managers say that's why some picture houses keep open in the morning.

"What I need to get my pep back," he says, "is a little relaxation."

When he is through "relaxing," has he more enthusiasm to go back to work? No, he has less.

Years ago, William James taught that when you try to get things done you reach a fatigue point, where you don't seem to have enough energy to keep going. James insists that if you will only keep on through the hard place, you will find a new second wind of effort. Persist until you get your second wind.

Apply this rule of David Seabury's to every task: "I will keep on through the hard place until a new supply [of energy] comes to me."

In the Army air forces, when a man cracks up a ship but not himself, he goes back up immediately. They yank somebody out of a ship—so they can get him up at once. They don't send him out to the pictures; they send him up in the air.

Do you remember the time Ruth Nichols pulled a terrible crash and was in the hospital for weeks? She went up again before she could even walk; had herself carried to the field and lifted into a plane. Because she wanted to? No—but because she didn't dare to wait for fear to set in.

So when your sales talk cracks up, don't run away. Stay and face it. Go right back up into the air. Don't just make the usual number of calls—make twice the usual number.

"As a cure for worrying," said Addison, "work is better than whiskey." Also as a cure for "unenthusiasm"—to coin a much-needed word.

One Way to Get It Is to Catch It

Rule 3: Expose yourself to enthusiasm. Enthusiasm is as contagious as measles, so go around with people who are enthusiastic and you are bound to catch it. Shun those who are morose, who lack fervor, who drag their feet and their minds around the dull routine of daily duties.

When Walter R. Jenkins was New York representative of the magazine *Comfort,* he occasionally used to visit the home office in Augusta, Maine, where I was employed. After he had shaken hands, he usually started off the conference with this request: "Don't tell me any bad news. Don't tell me anything that is going wrong. Just give me the good news." The things we worried about might have wrecked his morale —and most of them never happened, anyway!

Rule 4: Be healthy. A sick salesman can hardly be an enthusiastic salesman.

Here's the Best Rule of All

Rule 5: To become enthusiastic, act enthusiastic. This is by far the most important of all the rules.

Just as the way to be brave is to act brave, the way to become enthusiastic is to *act* enthusiastic.

How do you act enthusiastic? Well, here are some of the outward signs of enthusiasm.

Fervor. This really means "heat." Warm up to your subject.

Intensity. Show it in appearance, in tone, in words.

Animation. When you talk, don't slump. Sit up, lean forward in your chair.

Gestures. There is nothing like the use of gestures to help a man talk with enthusiasm. Use gestures not for the effect of gestures on your prospect but for their effect on you.

Contact. Look at your prospect as though you had something important to say to him. The salesman who looks out the window or at the floor isn't displaying enthusiasm.

Energy. Put energy behind what you say. Say it positively. Avoid "word whiskers" like "uh" and "er."

It's All in Your Hands

Rule 6: Force yourself to act enthusiastically. Many sales-men are unenthusiastic because they are lazy. They could easily be enthusiastic if they would take the trouble. Shake yourself out of your inertia. Give yourself an occasional pep talk. If your prospect starts to go to sleep, don't prod him—prod yourself.

Remember the great slogan in Dorothea Brande's book "Wake Up and Live": "Act as if it were impossible to fail."

These are the rules. They work—they work miracles. Will it pay you to increase your enthusiasm?

George N. Quigley, manager for the Manufacturers Life Insurance Company in Los Angeles, said in his company's *News Letter:* "Enthusiasm is the one thing a buyer can't resist. Pause for a moment and recall the last five salesmen who called on you. From which one did you buy? Wasn't it from the fellow who was genuinely excited about his product and what it would do for you? The prospect reflects like a mirror the exact attitude of the salesman. If you are not excited about your selling, how can you expect him to be?"

Selling Maxims

Inaction evaporates enthusiasm.
The more you sell, the more you can sell.
Nothing great was ever achieved without enthusiasm.

CHAPTER TWENTY-EIGHT

Why Aren't You Selling More?

The greatest of all faults, I should say, is to be conscious of none.
—CARLYLE.

Many salesmen ask themselves "Why am I not selling more?" but few stop to answer. Salesmen do not answer because they have never really *thought* about it.

Most human beings would rather suffer than think; most salesmen would rather lie down and die than think! Ask the average salesman why he isn't selling more and he will give you the answer instantly—trust a salesman to have a ready answer! But generally it is as wrong as it is ready.

Why? Because the salesman does not think.

Every person in the world who is endowed with a brain should regularly take off a few minutes each day to think. He should have what Henry L. Doherty used to call a "brain sweat." As Arnold Bennett said (in a book that every salesman should own, "How to Live on Twenty-four Hours a Day"): "We do not reflect. I mean that we do not reflect on the genuinely important things . . . upon the main direction we are going. . . . Conduct can only be made to accord with principles by means of daily examination, reflection, and resolution."

So determine to devote fifteen minutes each day to "examination, reflection, and resolution." Unless you guide this process you are likely to drift off into musing, daydreaming, woolgathering, bird's-nesting! To avoid waste of time and mental effort, follow some orderly method of directing your thoughts. The following questions should help you. Try to ask yourself a few of them each day.

Ask Yourself These Questions about Your Activities

I. Am I making enough calls? (How many are "enough"? In general, as many as you can crowd into the longest day you have the time and the strength to work.)

As a preliminary, ask yourself these three questions:

How many actual complete sales presentations did I make today?

Should I have made more?

Why didn't I make more? (Be brutal with yourself in answering this question. It may be all right to fool your sales manager but it is plain idiocy to fool yourself.) After you have asked yourself these basic questions, go to work to find out why you did not make more calls, by asking yourself these questions:

A. Do I actually *plan* my day's work?

1. When?

2. How? Is it done each day on some systematic plan—or helter-skelter? To be sure that your planning is systematic, ask yourself:

(*a*) On whom do I plan to call tomorrow?

(*b*) Why? (Maybe you ought to call on somebody else. Are you sure—and what makes you sure?)

(*c*) *When* will you call?

It's Your Time—But Why Waste It?

The next step in the direction of getting more calls made is to ask yourself:

B. Do I waste time?

1. Do I start early enough?

(a) At what hour did I start making calls?

1'. Today?

2'. Yesterday?

3'. What is the average time, through the past month, that I have started to make calls?

(b) Why did I not start earlier?

1'. On whom could I have called earlier? (Most salesmen waste hundreds of productive hours because they delude themselves with the idea that calls cannot be made until such and such a time. Why fool yourself? The chances are 50 to 1 you can effectively start making calls much earlier than you do now.)

2'. Why don't I start earlier? (Face this question honestly. Don't rationalize, don't excuse yourself.)

2. Do I eliminate unnecessary traveling?

(a) Today, for example, did I waste any time in going from prospect to prospect when I could have used it more effectively in talking with prospects?

(b) Do I try to cut down lost motion?

1'. Do I work reasonably near home? (Assuming, of course, that it is possible to do so.)

2'. Do I work in one neighborhood, city, or territory? (That is, do I avoid jumping around?)

3'. Do I avoid unnecessary trips to the office or to the hotel?

4'. Have I eliminated customers so remote that it doesn't pay to call on them?

Look for the Time Wastes

3. Do I waste time around the office or hotel?

(*a*) Do I come in too often?

(*b*) Do I stay too long?

(*c*) What can I do to break myself of this bad habit?

4. Do I work late enough? (A failure of salesman since the beginning of selling has been to quit too early in the day.) Do *you* quit too early?

(*a*) In the last six days, what time (on the average) did I finish my last call?

(*b*) If I had really tried, could I have made just one more call?

(*c*) As a rule, what time do I quit working?

1'. Why do I quit at that time?

2'. On whom could I have called later, if I were really trying to do a full day's work?

5. Do I make night calls? (Obviously, night calls are impracticable for salesmen in certain lines. If your line is something that could be sold at night, you will probably find that one night call is worth two or three daytime calls.)

(*a*) When did I make my last night call?

(*b*) On how many nights have I made calls in the past month?

(*c*) Honestly now, am I making enough night calls—as many as I possibly can?

(*d*) How can I arrange to make more night calls?

6. Do I make enough calls on Saturday? Do I work all day, half a day, or not at all? Why? Are prospects available on Saturday? Do I have enough strength to work on Saturday? Is the salesman theory that salesmen should rest on Saturday based on sound reasoning, fear, or old-fashioned laziness?

7. Do I make calls on holidays? (In some lines, holiday calling is impractical, in others—for example, insurance and real estate—holidays are better than ordinary days. In such lines of selling, if you must have your day off, work on the holiday and take some other day off.)

8. Do I throw away any of my selling time:

(*a*) By going to moving pictures?

(*b*) By friendly chats? (A garrulous salesman can easily waste hours each week in idle conversation.)

(*c*) By just sitting around?

After you are sure you are making enough calls, go on to the next questions:

Do You Deserve to Close Sales?

II. Do I make a good sales talk?

A. Do I learn all necessary facts about the prospect and his business before I attempt to sell him?

1. Do I get these facts, if possible, before I make the call? Or, do I take a chance of blundering on them?

2. Do I actually get the facts? (Stop right now and ask yourself, "How much do I really know about the problems of the people on whom I am going to call tomorrow?")

B. Do I offer goods that I believe will best serve my prospect (as opposed to goods that pay the best commissions)?

Just exactly what do you plan to offer the prospect you are going to call on tomorrow?

C. Do I really plan the sales talks I use? Do I think them out the night before? Do I refresh my mind immediately before I go in to see a prospect on these points:

1. What shall I say to arouse his interest?
2. What shall I say to make him *want* what I am selling?
3. What shall I say in closing?

D. Have I consciously and deliberately used the rules of selling over and over in my sales work until it has become second nature to use them?

E. Do I always get the prospect's attention by using one of the openers suggested in this book, or some other crasher that observes the rule for getting attention?

F. Do I always get and hold the prospect's interest?

1. Do I always tell the prospect how my goods or services will benefit him?
2. Do I try to hold his interest by keeping him in the picture?

G. Have I written out and worked over the conviction part of my sales talk until I am sure it is the best possible one for my goods?

1. Does the talk give or imply all the facts that the prospect should know about my proposition?
2. Does it contain plenty of examples?
3. Are the facts arranged in a logical order?
4. Are they tied together so that there are no places where the prospect will fall through and quit?

H. Do I regularly try to arouse the prospect's desire to own what I am trying to sell him? Obviously, in selling to purchasing agents the desire for your articles must be aroused not in the heart of the man who buys them but in that of the man who will use them.

1. Do I point out the prospect's want of, or need for, the goods I am selling?

2. Do I show him that my goods will supply this want?

3. Do I paint a word picture of his satisfaction or gratification as a result of owning my goods?

I. Do I close by contrasting the advantages and disadvantages of owning my goods as compared with my competitors' goods?

J. Do I get the order on a minor point, double question, or alternative proposal?

K. Do I use any of the sales helps provided by my organization—sales letters, kits, charts, illustrations, and the like?

L. Do I talk slowly, clearly, and understandably? Do I carefully select only words and terms which I am sure my prospect will understand?

M. Do I ask for the order often enough?

N. Do I observe the rules in answering objections?

O. Do I exaggerate? (You should understate.)

P. Do I talk too much? (Do I give my prospect a chance to talk? Do I ask questions? Do I give my prospect time to answer? Do I listen attentively and with a real show of interest to what he says?)

Are My Prospects the Best?

III. Do I call on good prospects? (That is, people who may reasonably be expected to buy?)

A. On whom am I calling from day to day?

1. Where did I get the list? Is it the best possible list for me to use, or could I, by a little effort, get a better one?

2. Am I calling on enough *new* prospects—am I spreading out my list?

(*a*) Where do I get the names that I am adding to the list?

(*b*) Do I "radiate"? That is, do I get my present customers to give me new prospects?

3. Am I calling often on old customers rather than paying visits to new ones?

4. Have I eliminated poor prospects?

(*a*) Prospects whose business is too small to be worth fooling with.

(*b*) Prospects who are so antagonistic that they will never buy from me.

Am I Thinking Right?

IV. Am I in the right mental attitude to be successful as a salesman?

A. Am I satisfied with the organization for which I am working? (If not, do something to improve conditions, or change to some other organization.)

1. Has the company I represent a good standing in the community and with the people to whom I am trying to sell goods? (If you have to apologize for your organization, don't work for it.)

2. Am I getting satisfactory sales cooperation from my organization?

(*a*) Am I supplied with all needed facts?

(*b*) Has my sales manager taught me all I ought to know about selling and about the product?

(*c*) If I go into a slump, is someone available to go out in the field and make some calls with me and find out what is the matter with me?

(*d*) Does my company supply satisfactory sales helps and visual aids—statistics, maps, kits, and the like? (You might also ask yourself if you are *using* them, because probably you're not.)

(*e*) Do I get cooperation from the sales department in keeping me sold on the organization and its products?

1'. Are my superiors enthusiastic?

2'. Do they hold enthusiastic meetings?

(*f*) Does the sales department stimulate the spirit of competition by contests and by other methods?

3. Am I satisfied with the goods or service which my organization is offering?

(*a*) Is there anything definitely wrong with anything that my company offers?

(*b*) Should my company offer anything else to complete the line?

4. Are our prices right? That is, are they fair in relation to the price of competing goods, quality and service considered?

If You Don't Love Selling, Leave It

B. Am I convinced that, all things considered, selling is for me the very best job in the world? (If you have been selling for at least six months and if the answer is No, then start right out looking for another job. You will never succeed unless you feel certain that you would rather sell than do any other work in the world.)

C. Do I honestly put my prospect's interests ahead of my own? Do I forget my commission when I am making a sales talk and think only of what the prospect will gain by the transaction?

D. Do I feel that I can serve my prospects better, all things considered, than anybody else possibly could? (To do this, you must know more about the prospect and his wants and needs than any other salesman. Do you?) You must know more about the goods you are selling than your prospect does and be better fitted to give advice than your competitor. Are you?

E. Do I honestly feel that I am offering the prospect the goods which beyond all others are best fitted for the prospect's needs? (If not, you are unfair to your prospect and yourself.)

F. Do I *expect* to make sales? Can I actually see myself making the sales? Would I be willing to bet on my ability to get the order?

G. Do I approach each sale in a professional spirit, that is, as a doctor faces a case? You can do this when you have a background of knowledge and of experience in handling similar problems. What are you doing to make yourself a professional salesman rather than an amateur salesman?

1. What books relating to my business or product have I read in the past year?

2. What business or trade magazines do I read regularly?

3. What else am I doing to learn more about my company's goods?

4. What am I doing to learn about my competitor's goods?

H. Do I waste too much time on poor prospects merely because they are friendly? Do I quit too easily on good prospects because they put up a hard fight? Do I get along with people?

1. Do the people I call on like me?
2. Do I like them?
3. Do they ever treat me discourteously? If so, is it my fault or theirs?

Ask Yourself These Questions, Too

V. Miscellaneous.

A. Is my appearance good?

1. Do I wear the best clothes that I can possibly afford, and perhaps a little better?

2. Are they neither too loud nor too somber?

3. Are my clothes always neatly pressed?

4. Is my linen always scrupulously clean?

B. Am I loyal—do I run my part of the business as if I owned it?

C. Do I really *think* about my own business problems and those of my company?

1. Have I some regular time and place for thinking about business?

2. Do I give it enough time?

3. Do I concentrate so that I think about business and nothing else?

4. Do I keep a record of the results of this thinking?

D. Do I keep in good health?

1. Am I careful not to eat to excess? Especially, do I eat little at breakfast and lunch?

2. Am I moderate in drinking and smoking?

E. Am I making as much money as I want to? If not, what am I doing about it?

F. What is my ambition as to my ultimate destination in

business? What do I want to become? Do I want to be a sales executive? What am I doing to arrive at this destination?

Selling Maxims

A fault is more easily found than mended.

The sale that is thought through in advance is more than half fought through in advance.

"Learn from yesterday's poor sales talks," to paraphrase James W. Barrett, "but don't worry about them. The chief cause of unhappiness is trying to make poor sales talks unhappen."

If you sold, ask yourself why—and try to repeat. If you failed, ask yourself why, and try not to repeat.

No man ever became a great salesman by luck.

"Nobody can give you wiser advice than yourself."—CICERO.

A good way to relieve the monotony of your job is to think up ways of doing it better.

CHAPTER TWENTY-NINE

How to Get Yourself Promoted

He who comes up to his own idea of greatness, must always have had a very low standard of it in his mind.

—RUSKIN.

Some salesmen have no higher ambition than to keep on being salesmen. If they are *good* salesmen, that is a worthy ambition.

Suppose, however, that you are one of those who want advancement. You are the man who steps forward and asks: "How do I get to be a sales manager?"

Here are some time-tried rules for winning promotion:

Rule 1: Know more about what you are doing than any other salesman.

Know more about your company, its history, its personnel, its aims, its principles, and its practices.

Know more about the product you are selling.

Know more about your competitors and what they are selling.

Know more about how to sell. Read all the books on selling that you can find. Read selling magazines. Read books on advertising, magazines about advertising.

Have lots of general information. Read books about economics, books about how surveys are made, about current topics. ("Where do I find time?" you ask. I don't know. But

247

I do know that most of the men who get ahead find the time—so you should.)

Rule 2: Demonstrate that you can do the three big jobs of sales management: (1) hire them, (2) train them, and (3) work them. How can you do it? Well, it depends on what kind of company you work for. If you are with a live, growing company that can use more salesmen, be on the lookout for men. One of the most thrilling jobs that falls to the lot of a sales executive is to hunt for men who will develop into salesmen.

If the nature of your job permits, get your manager to let you take one man under your wing. Pick him, train him, then put him over. By the time you have done that for two or three men, you will probably find the executives of your company ready to give you the first opening as a sales executive.

Rule 3: Set a good example.

No sales executive will promote a salesman solely because he is a steady churchgoer, a teetotaler, or a shining moral light. Equally, however, no sales manager will knowingly promote a salesman who

(*a*) Drinks to excess. (The test is, does he let drinking interfere with business?)

(*b*) Gambles to excess.

(*c*) Is notoriously loose morally.

(*d*) Is constantly and hopelessly in debt.

(*e*) Gets a reputation for exaggeration, fancy tales, or plain lying.

A sales manager must, whether he likes it or not, set an example for his entire force. He is not likely to be made a manager if he constantly and conspicuously sets a bad example.

Don't Be a Violet

Rule 4: Get out from under that bushel. You can't hope to be promoted if nobody ever hears of you.

How can you bring yourself to the attention of executives? Well, here are some of the ways:

Work hard. It is always a good sign.

Make a lot of sales. You don't have to be a leader to win promotion, but you have to be a *salesman* and be ready to prove it.

Take an active part in sales meetings. The good sales executive is usually a good teacher. If you are, you can demonstrate it at meetings.

Be enthusiastic. No wise executive will ever promote to a sales-management job a man who is listless and sleepy.

Take a course in public speaking. Take the case of my friend Bo Webber. When he started his speaking course, he was last on his sales force. He had always been last. While he was taking the course, he went into first place. He never dropped out of first place. At the end of a year he resigned, took another job, and within another year was sales manager of the New York district for a large company.

When you learn to speak, get yourself invited to speak, at sales and advertising conventions if possible—in any event where heads of companies gather. If you do not bring yourself to the attention of your employer, you may bring yourself to the attention of somebody else who needs a sales manager.

Rule 5: Make suggestions—even if they are bad.

Rule 6: Keep everlastingly at it. A good job takes a lot of winning, but it is worth it.

Rule 7: Ask for it. Go to your boss and tell him you want the next executive job that opens up. Don't wait for it to open —or you may be too late.

When you ask, your immediate superior is likely to do one of three things:

(*a*) Tell you that you are hopeless and why. (If it's true, then it's time you knew.) If you are hopeless, it will probably be because you are lazy, cowardly, unenthusiastic, uncooperative, disloyal, because you lack executive or teaching ability, or because your morals are loose, or you drink or gamble too much.

(*b*) Tell you that you are not ready. In this case, have him tell you what to do to get ready.

(*c*) Tell you that he will consider you when the next vacancy occurs.

Selling Maxims

Brains never go out of style.

The successful salesman is a failure if he could become a successful sales manager—and doesn't.

Some salesmen are waiting for opportunity to break the door down and come in.

If you need a lot of managing, you'll never be a manager.

If you want to give orders, take orders.

Work faithfully eight hours a day and don't worry. Then, in time, you may become the boss and work twelve hours a day and do all the worrying.

CHAPTER THIRTY

Where Do We Go from Here?

Any fool can learn from experience. It takes a smart salesman to learn from a book—but it pays.

You didn't do quite your best yesterday, and the day before—what about tomorrow?

Unless you take some of the rules out of this book and make them a part of your daily selling life, I have wasted my time writing it and you have wasted your time reading it.

Again let me urge that you

1. Pick out the one rule in the book which you need the most.

2. Consciously and conscientiously use this rule in your day-to-day selling.

3. Keep on using it until its use becomes habitual.

4. Then move on to the next rule.

The rules in this book *work!*

I have been gathering them through almost a quarter of a century. All of them have been tried out—some of them by literally tens of thousands of salesmen under my supervision.

These rules are the rules that the winners use. They are the rules that bring in the orders. They are the rules that will increase your income and your chance for advancement.

If I can be sure that even a few of you who read this book will use even a few of the rules, I shall feel that I have not written in vain.

251

List of Visual Aids

The following list of visual aids may be used to supplement some of the material in this book. It is suggested that each film and filmstrip be previewed before using, as some may contain information that is too advanced or too elementary.

These films and filmstrips can be obtained from the producer or distributor listed with each title. (The addresses of these producers and distributors are given at the end of this listing.) In many cases these visual materials can also be obtained from your local film library or local film distributor; many universities have large film libraries from which these films can be borrowed.

The running time (min), whether it is silent (si), or sound (sd), whether it is color (C), and whether it is a motion picture (MP) or filmstrip (FS) are listed with each title. All of the motion pictures are 16mm; filmstrips are 35mm.

Each film and filmstrip has been listed only once in connection with the chapter to which it is most applicable; however, in many cases they may be used advantageously in connection with other chapters.

Chapter III—Making Habit Your Slave

Stepping Ahead in Salesmanship (College of the City of New York 30min sd FS). Shows the importance of growing, applying oneself, and developing the desire to get ahead.

Chapter IV—Five Steps of the Selling Process

Two Cents' Worth of Difference (Eberhard Faber 38min sd MP). A picture on the technique of salesmanship. It shows operation and organization of a sales force.

Chapter V—How to Gain Favorable Attention

Chapter VI—Additional Rules for Gaining Attention

The Right Approach (College of the City of New York 30min sd FS). Shows how to approach a prospect and the necessity for a plan.

It's the Little Things that Count (Bates 30min sd MP). Shows the problem of the retail salesman in reaching the buyer and gaining his confidence. Shows problems of retail merchant in getting the salesmen to conserve and plan their time.

Chapter VII—How to Arouse a Prospect's Interest

Chapter VIII—Some Additional Rules for Getting Interest

Handling the First Interview (College of the City of New York 30min sd FS). Shows the importance of the first interview; headlining the sales talk; concentrating on the features that interest him most.

Chapter IX—How to Convince Your Prospect

Presenting Values (College of the City of New York 30min sd FS). Shows methods of justifying price for the company's product.

Step-Up-and-Sell (C. P. Cochrane Co. 30min sd C FS). Shows that good salesmanship is based on keeping in mind the interest of the customer and selling only what the customer needs and is interested in.

Chapter X—How to Build a Sales Talk

Remember the Little Guy (Pepsi-Cola Co. 30min sd FS). Problems in selling the large store as contrasted with selling the small store.

Plan to Win (College of the City of New York 30min sd FS). Shows the need for an orderly, systematic procedure in approaching the selling problem.

You're the Doctor (Montgomery Ward 30min sd FS). Shows how to use suggestive selling.

Along Main Street (Coca-Cola Bottling Plants 30min sd FS). Shows the need for salesmen to take into account the human factors involved in selling.

Chapter XIII—How to Arouse Desire

Nobody Else but You (College of the City of New York 30min sd FS). Tells how the salesman has to rely on his own resources; how to apply imagination to the sales job.

Chapter XV—Secrets of Closing

Getting the Name on the Line (College of the City of New York 30min sd FS). How to follow through on a sale until the deal is completed; methods of closing.

Through to the Close (College of the City of New York 30min sd FS). Shows the technique of closing a sale.

Chapter XIX—If You Are Turned Down, What?

It Can Happen to You (Montgomery Ward 30min sd FS). Shows accidents that can and do happen to sales.

It's a Pleasure (Cooper's, Inc. 30min sd FS). Analysis of wrong retail selling techniques and their correction.

Chapter XXI—How to Answer Objections

Chapter XXII—Five Ways of Answering Objections

Chapter XXIII—Some General Rules for Answering Objections

First Olive (Jewel Tea Co. 30min sd FS). How to handle the customer who has changed his mind; excuses and objections and how they are handled.

The Woman in the Case (College of the City of New York 30min sd FS). How to handle the woman customer or the woman who goes along with the customer.

Chapter XXVI—Make More Calls

It's Your Business (College of the City of New York 30min sd FS). How to salesmanage oneself; being a salesman is like running one's own business.

Chapter XXVII—How to Become Enthusiastic

Sharper Shooting for Bigger Profits (Kelly-Springfield Tire Co. 30min sd FS). Sales methods in selling dealers; high-pressure methods.

How to Make a Sales Presentation Stay Presented (MTPS 30min sd MP). Shows sales force and dramatizes a successful sale.

General

How to Gather Honey Instead of Stings (Audi-Vision 15min sd FS). Presents the problem of criticism, indicating the desirability of omitting criticism unless it is absolutely necessary.

How to Get People to Like You (Audi-Vision 15min sd FS). Demonstrates the effect of genuine, active interest in other people.

How to Make People Want to Cooperate (Audi-Vision 15min sd FS). Shows how to influence cooperation by talking about what the other person wants and indicating how he can achieve his purposes by doing what you want.

How to Make People Appreciate You (Audi-Vision 15min sd FS). Illustrates the method of making people appreciate you by appreciating them.

How to Win Your Argument (Audi-Vision 15min sd FS). Indicates that if an argument cannot be avoided, it can be handled tactfully and courteously, preventing unpleasant disagreement.

How to Correct People's Mistakes Without Making Them Sore (Audi-Vision 15min sd FS). Discusses methods of praising before condemning, correcting the mistake indirectly, making the mistake seem small; emphasizes the importance of correcting mistakes in private.

How to Win a Sales Argument (MTPS 30min sd MP). Professors Borden and Busse of New York University act out technique of selling.

How to Remember Names and Faces (MTPS 30min sd MP). Importance of remembering prospects' names.

How to Make Your Sales Story Sell (MTPS 30min sd MP). How to dramatize your story.

Source of Films Listed Above

Audi-Vision, Inc., 285 Madison Ave., New York 17.

The Bates Manufacturing Co., Orange, N. J.

Charles P. Cochrane Co., Bridgeport, Pa.

Jewel Tea Co., Barrington, Ill.

Kelly-Springfield Tire Co., Cumberland, Md.

Lever Bros., 50 Memorial Drive, Cambridge 39, Mass.

Montgomery Ward, 75 Varick St., New York 13.

MTPS—Modern Talking Picture Service, 9 Rockefeller Plaza, New York 19.

Pepsi-Cola Co., 47-51 33 Ave., Long Island City, N. Y.

CCNY—College of the City of New York, Business Film Library, 17 Lexington Ave., New York 10.

Index

P

"People, The Art of Persuading," 101
Prejudices, handling of, 180-182
Printers' Ink, 59
Promotions, getting of, 247-250
Prospect, convincing of, 49, 53-74, 98
  interest of, in self, 34, 35
  getting in to, 202-216
Psychological moment, 130, 131
"Public Speaking as Listeners Like It," 78-81

Q

Questions, and orders, 151, 152
  for salesmen, 235-246

R

Realsilk, 60, 61
Refusals, minimizing, 168, 169
Rules, putting of, into practice, 10, 11

S

Sales, increasing of, 235, 246
Sales manager, becoming a, 247-250

Sales talk, building a, 76-88, 91-92
  checking a, 92-96
  memorizing a, 84-85
  preliminary work on a, 89, 91
"Secret of Closing Sales, The," 141
Selling maxims, 1, 2, 7, 12, 14, 15, 48, 75, 96, 97, 98, 99, 120, 123, 124, 171, 172, 185, 186, 193, 194, 203, 228, 234, 246, 250
Selling process, steps of, 13
Speaking, Dale Carnegie Course in Effective, 81
Speaking clearly, 62, 63

T

Trial closes, use of, 133-135, 138
Turndowns, handling of, 164-170
Twain, Mark (Samuel Clements), 63

W

Weighing advantages and disadvantages, 144-147
Word pictures, painting of, 111-113